Funny You Should Ask

MOSTLY SERIOUS ANSWERS TO MOSTLY SERIOUS QUESTIONS ABOUT THE BOOK PUBLISHING INDUSTRY

Barbara Poelle

WRITER'S DIGEST MAGAZINE COLUMNIST AND LITERARY AGENT

WITH A FOREWORD BY HOLLY ROOT, FOUNDER OF ROOT LITERARY AGENCY

WRITER'S DIGEST
BOOKS

 Published by Writer's Digest Books, an imprint of Penguin Random House LLC. First edition.

www.penguinrandomhouse.com

1 3 5 7 9 10 8 6 4 2

ISBN-13: 978-1-4403-5507-3

Edited by Amy Jones
Designed by Liz Harasymczuk
Cover Illustration by Bob Eckstein

Dedication

For Mom and Dad
Who always thought I could.
And for Travis
Who always thought I would.

Acknowledgments

None of this could be possible without Jessica Strawser, Tyler Moss, Cassandra Lipp, Baihley Gentry, and Ericka McIntyre—the editorial team both past and present at *Writer's Digest* magazine, which had the day-drinking brainstorm to give me a permanent column and have allowed me to get away with a lot ... and also very, very little. ("Ugh, just ... just give her back the turducken as an olive branch.") And a very loud and slightly weepy thank you to the inexhaustible Amy Jones, book editor extraordinaire; I have never worked so hard for an "lol" in a margin in my life. (I am *thirsty* for those lols.) Thank you also to Bob Eckstein, for a cover that is as spectacularly conceived and executed as I could have ever hoped for. Thank you to Liz Harasymczuk for incorporating the cover art into a great design and to Dana Kaye of Kaye Publicity who has kept me as hopping as she has laughing. To Death Kitten, Wombat, and the Scourge, aka Holly Root,

Abby Zidle, and Janet Reid, please don't tell anyone that you are the real brains here and I am basically made of cookie dough and spirit fingers and am easily distracted by shiny things.

Thank you to Irene Goodman—you called a girl on a run in Central Park and changed her life—and the sisterhood of the traveling insanity that is our agency, Miriam, Kim, Victoria, and Whitney; and Maggie Kane for without whom I kinda cannot do my job … or my life, really—("Maggie! My computer won't work." "Uh, it's unplugged." "Yeah, but shouldn't it still work?" [Incredulous pause] "It's not a lap … it's not … just … just don't unplug it again.")

Thank you to James Brandon ("Huh, I guess this is how it all turns out.") and James Bock ("And let that be a lesson to you, kid.") for being early readers and making sure that I was covering as much of the journey as I could, and for laughing. (I am telling you. So thirsty for those lols.) Thank you to Kelly Ceynowa who, through this book and through life, has carefully held my hand, my hopes (and okay, yes, fine, that one time in Cabo, my hair) since we met in preschool. And to Amy Cobb who constantly works out my comedy muscles—and my stomach muscles—by being exponentially funnier than me. ("That first step'sa doozie.")

Thank you to my parents who have always stood in unconditional support, and sometimes slightly bewildered laughter, of their I-saw-this-in-a-cartoon-once-I-think-I-can-do-it daughter, and to my sister, Andee, who was my first and forever lol'er.

To my clients, thank you for sharing your talent, your time, your tears, your hopes, your disappointments, your dreams, your disasters, and your lives with me. I cannot express to you the privilege and joy it is to facilitate your careers, to know you. I am constantly in awe of you, and I am so grateful to be a part of your art.

To Charlotte and Sylvia, all of this is for you. All of it.

And finally, to Travis … and Travis … and Travis …

And Travis.

About the Author

Barbara Poelle works as a literary agent and lives in New York City with her husband, Travis, and her two ferocious daughters.

Table of Contents

Foreword

When I first met Barbara Poelle in 2007, I'm fairly sure I gave her nothing more than a frosty "nice to meet you" before turning, pointedly, back to my keyboard. You see, when we met we were both newly minted literary agents whose companies shared an office space, and in the parlance of reality television circa the early aughts, I was not there to make friends. Coming off a stint at an agency whose workplace culture one might politely describe as "intense," I had no reason to think the overly peppy blue-eyed lady in the cubicle down the way was anything but a distraction from the ultimate goal: publishing world domination.

I wore my newness like a scarlet letter, something to be hidden and shed as quickly as possible. Barbara embraced hers, bounding toward new learning with the joy of a golden retriever puppy who just saw a squirrel for the first time. While I panicked each day that I was about to be fired (by whom, exactly, or why was unclear—but let this not be a barrier for the Type A in search of a worry), Barbara exulted in the daily discoveries of mastering a new professional stage. The joy she took from every new experience was contagious, and soon her chilly, panicky officemate (me) couldn't resist inching a little closer, won over by her enthusiasm, yes, but also the undeniable fact that she had the goods. Her taste and instincts were impeccable, and I couldn't resist the pull of her orbit. Maybe I could be there a little to make friends?

The quirks of New York City office real estate soon led to us literally sharing an office, giving us an excellent opener at publishing cocktail parties, where we frequently wingwoman-ed one another through editor encounters ranging from sublime to excruciating: "We're officemates!" one of us would say, setting up the other to chime in, "But we don't work for the same agency!" But more importantly, with this greater proximity something wonderful happened: I discovered that the peppy blue-eyed lady wasn't a distraction from world domination; she was the key. The lead balloon (me) and the helium zeppelin (her) helped each other find the perfect cruising altitude. And together, both of our careers took flight.

In the years that followed, we have celebrated many career highs (and weathered a few lows—we're magnificent at our jobs, make no mistake, but we're still humans working in publishing). We've sat in companionable silence reading manuscripts for most of many weekends, breaking only for snacks and refills delivered by one or the other of our bemused husbands. We've closed down the Javits Center at the end of Book Expo and toasted the opening of my agency. We've compared submission lists, tried to build a better publishing mousetrap (the mice are slow and resistant to change, but swapping cheese for peanut butter is worth a try!), and fought arm in arm to better an industry we believe in, because whatever the differences in our approach at the outset, we were always united by our belief that books can absolutely change the world. She is still the first person I text with a sticky work situation, a contract negotiation gone sideways, or good news to be celebrated (believe me when I say no one—no one—is better at celebrations than Barbara Poelle). It is no exaggeration to say my career is what it is today thanks to her insights, advice, and support. Where I once would've seen only the challenges of a situation or glumly accepted the conventional publishing industry thinking, she gently pushed me to see opportunity and blaze a new trail. And I like to think I've helped her out a little bit too along the way (if only by hissing at a few key junctures "It's called

GOOGLE, Poelle"—then promptly answering the question because by now I've truly embraced and accepted my calling as her own personal search engine).

So you can see, Dear Reader, why I am truly overjoyed that she has written this book. These pages you hold are the closest thing I can picture to capturing the experience I was so fortunate to enjoy lo those many years ago, though I hope you'll learn from my errors and accept that resistance to the Way of the Poelle is truly futile. Best to embrace it and prepare, instead: Select a beverage of your choosing, acquire some tasty snacks, and if historical accuracy is your thing and you want the full Holly experience, pretend you are sharing an office that was definitely once a storage closet. Then gird your loins and flip the page. As Barbara answers your publishing questions, you can count on receiving her wise and truly inimitable feedback—always honest, always encouraging, and very, very funny.

I don't know you personally, Reader, though I am confident you are very talented and I am also getting a strong vibe that those pants you've chosen today are really working for you, but even so I can guarantee you Barbara Poelle is cheering for you to become your very best writer-self and fully live into your potential as a storyteller. At every stage of her career, she's been an unwaveringly passionate advocate for authors, both hers and other agents' clients. I've seen her speak to the most nervous aspiring authors at conferences and parties with the very same laser-beam attention and respect she gives to CEOs of publishing houses (honestly, maybe more? As a group, authors are funnier, and funny counts for a lot with Poelle). She finds people fascinating, none more so than writers, and I have witnessed countless instances where the sheer power of her belief has transformed careers and lives. So it is no small thing for me to say: She is cheering for you. And therefore, because of the transitive property way our friendship works, I am too. Can you handle that much positive energy coming your way? I hope you're prepared to be amazing, because we've got high expectations for you.

Above all, I can promise if you take her words in these pages to heart, your journey through the fearsome wilds of publishing, like my own, will be much the better for it—and you'll laugh enough to scare away any beasts hiding in those woods. Are you ready? Let's get to it.

Holly Root
Founder, Root Literary
January 2020

Introduction

For the better part of a decade, I have been writing the Q&A column "Funny You Should Ask" in *Writer's Digest* magazine. Folks have been generous and vulnerable in writing in and asking about the traditional book publishing process and then allowing me to impart a bit of insight accompanied with wine sloshing, tuba sounds, and jazz hands. And thus, let us continue and expand! In the following pages you will find questions and answers to some of the most common quandaries that pop up when one is navigating the publishing world—along with some new vintages, brass instruments, and Fosse fingers. This is a guide for those just beginning to write, those prepared to query, those signing with an agent, and those several books into their career who spend a few nights a year screaming into a towel, "I am a big phony and everyone is going to discover I can't write and we'll lose the house and Janice will have to go back to night shifts at the rendering plant." Since I can't represent *all* of you, this will be a little slice of the pointers I would give you in a class or as my client—like if your eyeballs had me on speed dial. While no two publishing paths are alike, this should cover the basics, hopefully with a few chuckles on the way. Because all of this is hard. All of this is disorienting and sometimes outright humiliating.

In fact, I wish there were reference guides like this for other aspects of life as well. Recently I was meeting an editor for drinks in Tribeca, and when I arrived at the establishment and opened the outer vestibule door, windblown and off balance, I immediately noticed a pay phone prominently featured on the wall.

Ugh. I haaaaate this. The fake speakeasy. Where you have to have a password, or enter a phone booth and find the secret latch. It is just so annoying.

I made eye contact through the glass with the young man standing behind the host podium in the restaurant, maybe twenty feet away. I rolled my eyes and picked up the phone. A tone sounded saying "Press nine!" And I did, and nothing happened. I maintained eye contact with the host who was calmly half smiling at me through the glass, pressed 9 again. And again. I blew some errant strands of hair out of my eyes and then just started yelling through the glass, "Look, I am pressing nine and nothing is happening, can you just buzz me in or whatever?" He just continued to smile, which now appeared to me like a smirk. So I yelled through the glass, "I don't know what to do, and I quite frankly don't care, can you just let me in already? I don't have time for this and even if I did I would still be annoyed!" And then … a thought occurred. And a gentle flop-sweat volcanoed out from my scalp. I slowly, still maintaining eye contact, set the pay phone back in its cradle. And tried the door. Which was open the whole time. Because this was *not* a speakeasy bar. I had seen the pay phone and assumed it was. So, still maintaining eye contact with the host, I ascended the steps to the stand, which was the longest twenty-foot walk I ever had. When I got to him, his smirk deepened, and he said lightly, "Well *that* was fun."

So while you are on this journey, there will be times when you are the host … and there will be times when you are a middle-aged white woman, hair askew, screaming through the glass at a stranger. But, he was right: this *is* fun. Educating and equipping yourself for the journey will add such important tools to your writer's toolbox, and this book can be part of that. No two journeys in life are the same, thus no two journeys in publishing will be either. Nothing in here should be assumed to guarantee your success—it is not a how-to—it is more like a lantern to shine in the darker unknowns of the basics of the publishing journey. Then, when you are confident in the basics you can start to find the fun and avoid some of the common pitfalls and pratfalls along the way. There will be a lot of advice and anecdotes in the following pages, but if I can start and end with the most valuable, it is, of course, in writing and in life:

Try the door first.

Because now? Now the real work begins.

PART 1

Once when I was at the Museum of Modern Art, I passed an installation that consisted of crumpled facial tissues spilling out of a sideways garbage can. I turned to my friend and fellow literary agent, Janet Reid, and said, "This? Why is this art? I mean, *I* could do this." And she replied, "But you didn't." So first and foremost if you are reading this book because you are *writing* a book, congratulations. You are *doing* it. And one man's crumpled tissue is another woman's six-week installment at a famous museum, so there are all kinds of needs for all kinds of audiences. But no matter what you are writing, craft is everything.

Craft is the technique and detail work in sentence—and therefore story—structure. It's the color choice *and* brush strokes of your book ... and it's also the stuff that makes you Edvard Munch in the mirror at five in the morning saying "I wonder if I can get my job back at the sod farm."

When crafting, I cannot stress the importance of connecting with a writing group and/or critique partners (CPs). They are your first readers, and the ones that will quickly learn your tricks and cheats and follies and foibles, and bust you on them. I personally believe (although I am proven wrong from time to time) that your CPs cannot share fluids with you in real life: no girlfriends, boyfriends, spouses, siblings, parents, or children, because those types of relationships bring a nuanced history along with every read, for better and for worse. (I will allow first cousins, however, because growing up, was anyone more aggressive yet more dependable than a cousin?) You need someone who will be thrilled about what is working, but pointed about what needs to go, because craft consists not only of creating, but destroying. Stephen King teaches us that in his must-have resource *On Writing* with the phrase "Kill your darlings," and I echo that on a weekly basis with my clients.

The craft of killing our darlings is the difference between:

> Barbara stepped gingerly into the room, her shoulders hiked up around her ears, her breath held as if in precursor of some catastrophe; modern art made her nervous.

and

> Barbara stepped into the room and exhaled; modern art made her nervous.

Both sentences are crafted to put us in the where and who and what and when of the story, but the second one does it with less, and will create and sustain the pacing and establish the rhythm moving forward.

While we are crafting and killing and screaming and occasionally remembering to shower, remember that every book you see on a shelf comes from an author who did the same. This can be a lonely journey, but it is one the village takes with you nonetheless. At the end of this book, there is a series of exercises that might help you in any point of your process, whether that is getting started with an idea, finding that needed fulcrum in the center of the novel, or loosening that sticking place in the penultimate scene without making *the whole thing a dreeeeeam.*

Even though, it kinda is, isn't it.

But let's get to it, because now? Now the real work begins.

Dear FYSA,

In my middle-grade novel, some of my protagonist's dialogue reflects conversations I've had with my nine-year-old nieces. Yet critiques suggest that my voice in those instances is not correct for my protagonist (of like age). I am confused about how what a child said to me in real life wouldn't come across as a child's voice in writing. What are your thoughts?

Sincerely,
Dialogue Dumbfounded

Dear Dumbfounded,

I hear you. I recently texted my husband about a shade of bath towel I wanted, and why he needed to specifically get that shade and what that exact shade reminded me of. He was with our two children in Bed, Bath & Beyond, which is like bringing goats to a roller rink, and he sent me back a series of emojis that could only be truly appreciated by stevedores and acrobats. I think we're in the same boat here, which is that this has more to do with tone and structure than actual syntax, and more about how the musicality translates into reality by the reader than about real-time conversations.

Overall, dialogue in a novel or film is simply tighter, better, and more universally accessible than in real life. (For instance, start counting the *ums*, *uhs*, and *likes* in your own conversations). Dialogue in fiction has to move the plot along in some way or the pacing gets all wonky (a technical publishing term you need years to learn) so it has to be curated to a degree. In the case of an adult author translating a middle-grade protagonist, (though it would be easier for me to see the actual dialogue in question to fully weigh in) there can be a few other factors that might make it come off as disingenuous.

When you look at the construct of a youthful character voice, the absence or presence of slang can be a determining factor in accessibility. Sometimes "peer speak" can be off-putting in a novel, whereas other times it's necessary to achieve realism—but this would be based on the tone of the discourse already established.

Beyond that, cultural background, region, and even neighborhood can and will influence *all of us* in dialogue and kids are no different. "You fixin' for a coke?" means the same thing as "You gonna grab a pop?" only a few hundred miles away. What resonates as "normal" conversation in one region of America might sound stilted in another. Also, one nine-year-old's commentary can be another fifteen-year-old's inner monologue—so perhaps the education, background, and maturity of these particular nine-year-olds in your life do not resonate with how the majority of their peer group converses.

In the end, hearing from more than one source that the voice comes across as inorganic has more to do with the rhythm of the work than the field research behind it. Keep eavesdropping (I mean, for a variety of reasons, obvi) but *keep reading the genre.* That will help to grow your data set and tap into where the art meets the life.

Dear FYSA,

I realize it depends on many things—such as audience, characters, and genre—and also understand that repeated usage goes into the law of diminishing returns. But my question remains: How much smutty language is appropriate? One f-bomb in a novel can turn off entire segments of readers, but it can also express a character's intense feeling or reaction. Is there a rule of thumb?

Sincerely,
Pondering Profanity

Dear Pondering,

Hmm. As the occasional holler throughout my apartment "*MAMA USED A LAZY WORD*" might attest—I tend to, uh, work the room a little "blue" myself, so I may not be the best barometer. However smutty is a pretty subjective line in the sand. Your smut might be my word-a-day calendar.

For example, the first line of Andy Weir's *The Martian* is probably one of my favorites insofar as setting up tone, tension, and character, but some folks would immediately put the book down after that sentence. In the middle of a difficult negotiation, I have been known to hang up the phone and then howl a stream so profoundly offensive that there is a rule in my office that I am not allowed to swear before 10 A.M. EST. (This is true.) Yet, ask me to read a steamy passage from the brilliant and ferociously sexy Christina Lauren novels and I will clutch my pearls and eyeball the nearest fainting couch because "Well I never!" and collapse with great fanfare. [*Peeks open one eye, turns back to page, continues reading.*]

Even so, for as "Well, my *stars* and *gardens*!" as I can get, (I say *gardens* because *garters* is just so smutty! Nah, I say gardens because that's totally what I thought it was until my editor told me it was garters. But ... STET!) it's never really about being offended. I'm much more apt to be offended by misinformed concepts or gratuitous plotlines than actual dialogue or prose. And I am 100 percent likely to be offended by appropriation of and stereotypical depictions of characters or cultures. But as far as profanity goes in written work, I'm more likely to be bored by the lack of creativity from an author who loads the T-shirt cannon with f-bombs and launches them indiscriminately into a manuscript than to find myself disgusted by a narrative. Hence why we call them "lazy" words in my house. There are sooooo many words, picking something without using the big seven (nod to Carlin) asks for a little more from the source, and can be even more horrifying and satisfying in its ability to peel the paint off the walls.

In the end, as long as you aren't writing, say, middle-grade inspirational novels, I would simply suggest you stay true to the voice of your characters and allow them to set the tone. If it's true to the story, your readers will go right along with it. And if they don't like it, they can [air siren] up their [old-timey car horn] and [broken spring sound effect].

Dear FYSA,

What is women's fiction?

Signed,
Genderly Interested

Dear Interested,

Women's fiction is a nebulous term that can encompass subgenre elements like fantasy, magical realism, crime, and romance. The main distinction of women's fiction is that the themes and issues within the novel are associated with/directed at and therefore marketed to, women.

Let's all take a minute and roooollll our eeeeeeyes at the notion that all women clearly have the same life experiences and therefore resonate with common themes. And as there is no corresponding category for men's fiction (those are just called *novels* [sound of smashing]), popular fiction, commercial fiction, mainstream fiction, and general fiction also can define and understand the audience and intent behind most women's fiction. Themes like empowerment, survival, and loss are explored in women's fiction and can be executed in a more commercial voice or a more upmarket or literary narrative—like any other mainstream novel.

The reason we use classifying terms like *women's fiction* is to help to establish the main marketing pool, but that doesn't mean those are the only waters your novel can swim within.

Dear FYSA,

If a fantasy novel by an unpublished writer is 150,000–160,000 words, does that affect its chances of getting published? I don't mean a badly revised story, but a good story that needs many words to be told. Guidelines often say that 120,000 words is the maximum, but a lot of fantasy novels are much longer. Is publishing long novels a privilege of well-known authors only?

Thanks very much,
Andrea of Avalon

Dear Avalon,

I was once in a very high-end restaurant and the waiter brought a slice of key lime pie to our table. My friend and I continued to chat as we each sank a fork into the pie and while he was still talking I placed the fork in my mouth and … you know that scene in the movie *The NeverEnding Story* where it cuts to Bastian on Falkor's back and he throws his fist up and screams a joyful "YEAHHH!"? That is what every single one of my taste buds did. The pie was the perfect combination of tart and sweet with a flaky, flirty crust but heavy, demanding homemade whipped cream. It was a combination impossible to achieve. And that is what you must strive for, in any genre, but especially in fantasy. Every word has to fall in line with the world building, the rules of that world, and the construct of the characters' backstory and slang, peer speak and dialogue specific to those three components. So yes, there *are* certain genres, such as science-fiction and fantasy, that allow or even demand a higher word count. But you want your reader to have a minimal amount of chewing for the maximum flavor.

Because fantasy depends so heavily on world building, it is very important for the author to that the reader knows the "rules" of that world. When I see a debut fantasy novel that rings in upwards of 135K, my experience has taught me that the world building has consumed the narrative. (Also let us not forget, that is *very* expensive for the publisher to create, and they are looking for the maximum return on investment, and their executives are going to have a hard time believing an untested novelist is the right time to invest that money in production cost.)

Also, I balk at your above use of the word *privilege*, because it's actually an earned right. There's a sense of trust between a reader and an established author: They've been at the dance together before, so readers are more comfortable being led down the narrative lines of a lengthier work. With a debut, you need to work a little harder for a date, so it's best for the story to be as well-groomed as possible. Like I say, (stealing directly from Janet Reid and not crediting her) you can prepare to be the exception, but don't plan for it.

Dear FYSA,

Would my novel be classified as historical fiction if the story has historical figures and events, but they're secondary to the plot?

Sincerely,
The Ghost of Fiction Present

Dear Ghost,

Don't underestimate how much influence those historical elements have on your story. Time period and atmosphere have a way of becoming ingrained in the other key story elements and thus are rarely, if ever, "secondary to the plot."

Historical fiction, in plainest terms, is a novel set in a historical setting. I would challenge you to tell me any book written in a historical or nostalgic time period (the term often used for books that take place in the recent past, but the past nonetheless) that wasn't directly influenced and supported by the time it was set in, otherwise why would the author feel the pull to do so?

Historical fiction can also be a subgenre of a larger category, as with historical romance, which encompasses love stories that are undeniably influenced by the historical context. So even if your story is primarily a mystery, thriller, coming-of-age tale, etc., it never hurts to specify it as "historical" so that you and your potential future agents and publishers can envision where your novel should be shelved.

Still unsure? The best way to discern where your book fits in is to read comparative titles already on the shelf (which you should be doing anyway, for a whole host of other reasons). If you need help finding them, depend on the stalwart genius of your local librarian. These are the book knowledge *ninjas*. Sashay over to the public library, describe what kind of book you're writing and ask if there is anything similar in theme, tone, character, or plot like that on the shelves—those are your comparative titles. Then see how those comp titles are categorized.

Also—and I know this may get a little chicken bones and sage for some—as I encourage my clients to do, go to the exact spot in the bookstore, categorically and alphabetically, that your novel would likely be shelved, and imagine your book between the copies to the right and the left of it. Then? Buy and study those two books that would sandwich your title. They are in your target genre and made it to the same shelf—they are indeed comp titles. What you learn can help you become more confident in the way your work is both defined and distinguished moving forward.

Dear FYSA,

I'm having a hard time finding my comfort level in sharing my writing. I realize this sounds silly, since the goal of a writing career is obviously to be read—but if I were to have a book accepted by an agent or publisher, that would give me confidence that it had merit. As it is, I have no idea if my work is any good, and don't want to embarrass myself in front of people I know and respect if it isn't. But I recognize that I need feedback, and I'm reluctant to use an anonymous online critique forum because I want to know that the person who is offering me input is someone whose opinion I value. How can I get over this anxiety?

Sincerely,
Writing in the Dark

Dear Writing in the Dark,

So you want to write but don't want to be read. Wait. This is a PSAT question, isn't it? Okay, so it's like the farmer trying to get the bag of grain and the chicken and the fox across the river but his boat can carry only one item and he can't leave the fox with the chicken, or the chicken with the grain. I crushed the PSATs, I mean *crushed* them, so let me have a shot at this:

Place half of your manuscript in an envelope, and walk it to your neighbor's house while leaving the second half on the kitchen table …

No? Okay, how about this:

Find a reader you trust and lie to them, like, "Hey, this is weird, I know, but my Uncle Flart wrote a book and I really like it, but I think it's just because I like Uncle Flart—who had to overcome a lot of adversity, including being named Flart—so would you look at the first ten pages and let me know if it's something you'd read more of?"

Used that ruse before? Well then:

Remember in *Indiana Jones and the Last Crusade* when Indiana had to take the leap from the lion's head and he just closed his eyes, extended his leg and the path was *right there waiting to receive him*? Try that. Try just taking the first step.

Opinions have only as much power as you give them (including those from agents and editors, by the way—many times I've had my clients' projects passed over by multiple publishers before going on to find homes elsewhere and become big hits), but you should have a few trusted readers who understand your nervousness and will still be forthright. Start with one or two people immediately outside of your innermost circle of relationships, and just extend your leg and step. The path is right there, I promise.

Dear FYSA,

What types of character conflicts and plots are overdone in the submissions you're currently seeing? What would writers be well advised to avoid if they want to stand out?

Sincerely,
Fresh Face Forward

Dear Fresh Face,

Ever since Grok sat by firelight and grunted out *A Tale of Two Saberteeth* (yes, I'm certain the plural of sabertooth is saberteeth—don't interrupt me!) people have been telling basically the same story: A protagonist has a conflict, uses a mental and tactical skill set to solve it, and evolves from the experience. (Ironically, Grok himself wouldn't evolve for another 80,000 years.) The variations on this theme come from the storyteller's unique perceptions and life influences, which serve to create originality within plot formats that otherwise sound vaguely familiar. So it's difficult to say, "Knock it off with the 'North Korea International Terrorism Plot,'" or "Enough with the 'Big-City Girl Returns to Small Hometown and Finds What She Was Looking for All Along.'" What I look for is a fresh take, someone bringing something new to the table, perhaps in the form of a unique skill set for the protagonist or a fresh backdrop for the plot. For instance, take one of those themes above, and imagine that the author set it in 1899. Or with an all-teen cast. Or in outer space.

The one thing I'd recommend against is choosing a plot *because* you think it will fit well into a trend. Yes, I know I said that technically nothing can be overdone if you have a fresh take, but—aside from the fact that the *current* trends are manuscripts that were acquired and sold up to eighteen months previously, and are therefore by definition *former* trends—if you begin your writing process by trying to write what you think publishers want, you're not writing from the right place. Your writing should feel like something you *have* to do or else you will get crabby and yell at the kids and throw coffee on your assistant. Writing should not be something you do by a spreadsheet based on hot trends or outlandish plotlines you have determined to be "unique."

Finally, the phrase "avoid if they want to stand out" seems like an oxymoron to me. Rather than things to *avoid* to stand out, there are things to *embody* to stand out, and they all involve the actual mechanics of writing—the plot being a foundation on which to build your voice and characters and the musicality of the read. Essentially, standing out is about focusing and educating yourself on the craft to make every word count.

Dear FYSA,

Is it wise to publish the rough draft of a novel online, either serialized on my own blog or posted to a public critique forum or writing community? Will this deter agents and editors from accepting the manuscript, even if it appears online only as a rough draft that will be rewritten? I have received answers on both ends of the spectrum—mostly from self-published writers—and would like an answer from an agent.

Best,
Web Leery

Dear Leery,

Huh. First, I'm of the thinking to *never* put *anything* out there in rough draft form. Ever. You are the only voice your work has, and to create a lukewarm readership on an incomplete execution does not do it fair justice.

But, I may be alone in this thinking, so if we're going with this scenario, here is how my experience unfolds:

You send me a query, I like it and request the full manuscript. If it's in messy draft form, I get bummed out and I say, "This is a great idea, but the execution isn't there." And I pass, and you have undermined your efforts by querying with a project that wasn't your best. (*Whyyyyy?*)

Or: The manuscript is a little rough in places, but all the right birdies and cherubs and St. Bernards wearing barrels of Polish vodka appear and after the last page I fall down twice on the sprint to the phone to beg you to be my client. After you accept, you say, "I serialized a draft on my blog and people seemed to like it!" And I say, "How many people?" And you say, "327,926," and I laugh and clap and dance and say, "Cool! You're going to need to take it down, though." Or you say, "Forty-seven people," and I still laugh and clap and dance because I love the book so much and I say, "Cool! You're going to need to take it down, though." Because I wouldn't want anything that isn't in its best form available. But will its having appeared online deter me from representing it? Nope.

Now, as far as online critique forums go—I think everyone should have a critique group or partner. They can help immeasurably. But I'd prefer that be done offline or in an invite-only online forum. Think of any sort of public viewing of your writing like this: Your manuscript needs you to come over and drink wine and set up its online dating profile to find its best match. You would *never* allow your novel to post a profile picture that adds ten pounds or sports a funny haircut, would you? Make sure when anyone has the chance to see it, it's in its finest light. You both deserve it.

Dear FYSA,

If you are interested in eventually branching out into multiple genres, and have initial success in a single genre, how do you know when it's a good time to try a different one?

Sincerely,
Genre Hopper

Dear Hopper,

Ah yes, the whole, *If Bo can know football AND baseball, why can't I?* question. (The cool kids are still making "Bo Knows" references, right? Nailed it.) And this is actually quite common. My author Cat Winters writes in multiple genres. So does Sophie Littlefield. Heather Herrman wrote the adult horror novel *Consumption* for Random House and then next delivered me a young adult novel which we sold to Penguin. Inversely, bestselling YA author Adrienne Young just recently delivered me a *dynamite* adult manuscript that I'm shopping to publishers now. I am all about branching out when the author can handle the scheduling. It's the "interested" that catches me up here. My experience has been that this often means that an author mistakenly believes that another genre is easier (people say that to me a lot about YA), or that she can write faster than the book-a-year pace her current publisher is committed to, or that skill in one genre would necessarily translate well to another. But the truth is, there is no *time* to try a different genre.

Wait, no, there is.

The time to try a different genre is when your muse kicks open your office door, stomps across the floor in her combat boots, blows a piece of her feather boa from where it was stuck to the corner of her mouth, grabs your head by the ears, and bellows, "There is this girl who has been told her whole life that she is so sickly that if she leaves her house she will die—but she has a crush on the gorgeous boy who lives next door and watches him all the time and one night his house catches fire and she goes out her window and into his to save him and … *What happens next???*" And then she pulls what appears to be a meatball sub from the front pocket of her overalls, bites into it, chews voraciously, belches, and walks back out.

That is the time.

When you are trying to finish your upmarket women's fiction, but you know you'll discover weird marinara stains on your doorknobs and the lingering smell of provolone belches hovering around your head until you write *that story* … that is the time to try a different genre. Your muse makes that call. Not the market.

Dear FYSA,

Do writers from Australia or the United Kingdom pitching their work to U.S. agents need to edit their manuscripts to reflect American spelling conventions?

Sincerely,
A Writer Abroad

Dear Abroad,

At point of submission? Nah. But personally I like to know right away in the query if someone is from elsewhere because sometimes I struggle with the comma thing. It seems there are slightly different rules for commas outside the United States, and my brain will fall over a comma that isn't there.

Like, say you had a settee in the same place for years and then you moved it to the other wall, and then you had a party, during which you stepped back to where the settee had been, and you think you will fall over it so you kind of windmill your arms and slosh your drink across three people and yell, "Here comes death!" That is what my brain does when there is a comma missing.

It will take me a few pages to be like, "Oh! Not an American writer," but before I realize this, my brain is pinballing and flinging vodka on potted plants. So for me, as long as it's clear in the query the writer is from another country, I can adjust accordingly before the read. Other than that, there really isn't a need to Americanize a manuscript at the point of submission. Now, if you have an American protagonist living in Ohio saying things like *trainers* instead of *sneakers* and *jumpers* instead of *sweaters*, we might revisit this conversation before I sign and shop the novel, but at point of submission, I just want to see something that makes me want to fling myself onto the settee and *read*.

Dear FYSA,

Do you have any tips for avoiding distractions while writing? I always find that when I really want to jot something down, everyone close to me is pining for my attention, almost as if they are jealous of the pen and paper.

Sincerely,
Annoyed Author

Dear Annoyed,

Oh, sister, I hear ya. There just aren't enough hours in the day, and let's be honest, if there *were* more, I would use them for sleeping.

Now trust me, I know what it's like to not even get to go to the bathroom by yourself, much less grab some QWERTY time, but I'm going to slap you around a little bit and say this: If you want it badly enough, you have to find the time.

Jamie Freveletti once told me she sets a timer before she goes online to promote on any social media platforms so that she doesn't get sucked in, and James Brandon turns off his Internet access while he writes. I have authors who have spouses/in-laws/neighbors who run the show for two hours a day every Saturday and Sunday so they can go to a library to write. If the munchkins are all over you, take your laptop and hide in the bedroom, the closet, the minivan (Hey, Sarah Lemon!), the pantry, and get 500 words in. Find a sitter for two hours, sacrifice an hour of sleep on the front and back end of the night, tell everyone you're in the National Guard and check into a hotel one weekend a month, invent cloning, or *do whatever you have to do* to take this seriously.

And if you aren't organically getting the support at home to be taken seriously in your need for time to write, try begging, bartering, or trading times with other working parents once a week. Suggest they use *their* alone time to nap. You'll have dozens of takers.

Dear FYSA,

Should I bother revising a key device in my novel in order to work with the agent of my dreams?

Sincerely,
Moonstruck

Dear Moonstruck,

When I was in sixth grade there was a boy whom I loved so much you could have called it a *pulverize* instead of a *crush*. Coming home from a field trip to the science museum, I happened to have the (Ode to Joy!) luck to sit in the seat in front of him for the long ride and overheard him telling his friend that he "could never like a girl in glasses."

Well. No problem!

I whipped off my glasses so fast a sonic boom echoed through the tri-state, and then I proceeded to have the confidence to turn around and engage him in what I am sure was classy yet accessible discourse for the remainder of the ride. Certain our *tête-à-tête* (on Super Mario Bros, maybe? or the follies of pinning our Guess jeans?) was the first step toward six years of bliss culminating as prom king and queen our senior year, before we both headed off to college where we would be campus darlings, I then preceded him off the bus ... where I couldn't see the steps, tripped, and exploded out of the doors as if I were launched from a cannon, my glasses flinging from my pocket and skittering across the pavement.

Suffice to say, writing to someone else's taste if it isn't your organic choice might be a dangerous and painful path. When you say you've been asked to revise "a key device," what does that mean exactly? Is it a case where you've been asked to consider changing from first to third person (which might be worth "bothering" to do)? Or is it, "I didn't like that they were angels—can you make them mermaids?" Or, "I think this would really work if it all took place in 1929 France instead of present-day Albuquerque"?

Who's to say this is the agent of your dreams, anyway? What is that criteria? I'm asking for real. What *does* that mean to you? Sometimes I get folks who say I am their dream agent and I wanna be like, "I once accidentally texted my client Tracy Kiely something a bit, um, *unsettling* because her name begins with the same three letters as my husband's. Was *that* part of your dream?" In my opinion, someone can only truly be identified as your dream agent after you've spoken to that agent—or several agents—and found that her career vision, working style, communication guidelines, work ethic, and overall enthusiasm matches your own.

In the end, there are a lot of variables that go into suggested revisions, and the extent and the supportive reasoning behind them. Changing a key component of your novel may fit your immediate needs, but as far as that dream agent? Just make sure you don't end up missing out on the other guy, the right guy, who thinks you're cute in your glasses.

Dear FYSA,

What do you like to read when you're not working?

Signed,
Betty Bookworm

Dear Betty,

Well, thanks for asking! Between me and you? I only *really* like reading thrillers, middle-grades, romances, YA novels, upmarket fiction, narrative nonfiction, commercial fiction, essays, literary fiction, poetry, magazines, novels in verse, novels in prose, classic novels, bestsellers in translations from other countries, subtitles, playbills, sides of cereal boxes, and damp newspapers blown up against wire fences.

I know—I'm pretty selective.

But this is a question I would spin back to you: What do *you* like to read—and I hope your answer includes writing reference books like Stephen King's *On Writing*, Anne Lamott's *Bird by Bird*, William Bernhardt's The Red Sneaker Writers series, and

James Scott Bell's *Plot and Structure*, all of which will help tremendously while you are crafting.

But I would also ask, when you read "for fun," is *that* the genre you're writing in? I've had instances where I've seen a manuscript from a prospective client focused on a genre (usually, for some reason, thriller) where the work comes so close to salable for me that I ask to see whatever he writes next. *Rinse. Repeat.* And there is usually a moment around submission No. 3 where I'm like, "Hold up. This person can write, but something isn't working." So I'll ask, "What do you like to read?" And dollars to doughnuts (I don't know what that means) the answer is usually not whatever genre he's been writing.

When I say, "Why don't you take a crack at writing that instead?" the next project is often the winner.

If you read a lot of Erik Larson, put that romance manuscript aside and start researching something. If you just reread a Jonathan Tropper novel, take a break from that thriller and start working on a family drama. I have a feeling *someone* reading this just had a light bulb moment. You're welcome. I'll take that dollar *and* your doughnut.

Dear FYSA,

A friend and I are wrapping up our final draft of a novel we wrote together. I can't seem to find any information on how to query a project that has more than one author. I get that most elements of the letter and pitch will generally be the same, but should the fact that it is a collaborative project be mentioned? How do I bring it up? Will the fact that it is more than one author make it harder to get an agent to want to represent the book?

Sincerely,
Copilot

Dear Copilot,

I do many Writer's Digest webinars with fellow literary agent and foreword-writer extraordinaire Holly Root. Basically what that consists of is A) Holly putting together a PowerPoint with accessible and educational slides, B) Holly creating a bulleted breakdown of talking points for the live presentation, and C) Holly writing a personal response to each participant who submits work for critique. My role is to A) Try to sneak slides of Ryan Reynolds or a monkey washing a cat into the PowerPoint, B) Explain how I don't think I should be required to wear pants if I'm not being *seen* on the webinar, and C) Write "Right, Hols?" in most of my comments on the critiques.

And I get the same credit.

So by all means, say there are two of you. Write the query exactly as you normally would (there's no need to specify which of you is writing the pitch, as presumably you both have input), and then highlight both of you equally in the author bio section.

Co-authorship will have no bearing on the appeal of the project itself to the agent.

But just make sure you're the Barbara. Those Hollys really seem to have to do a lot of work.

Dear FYSA,

I've been writing all my life. I was a creative director in advertising and have had my work published. So you would think I would know the basics by now—but the advice "Show, don't tell," has tripped me up for years. Doesn't the mere fact that you're writing mean that you're "telling"? Would you be so kind as to give examples?

Sincerely,
Tell It to Me Straight

Dear Tell It to Me,

I thought about how to reply, as this is one of the harder questions I've had to answer as a columnist for Writer's Digest. It was already after six P.M. in New York City, but I knew my stay-at-home husband would be fine with our two children a little bit longer, as this was nothing new: We've been happily married for fifteen years and I've been working full-time for the agency for most of that. I considered tapping into a little liquid intelligence in the form of vodka, which I always have close at hand.

Or:

I brought the phone to my ear, barely registering the 212 area code on caller ID. I already recognized the background sounds—like the monkeys were running the zoo. "Hey, babe," Travis said. "Doing my usual ETA call. Should we go ahead, or wait?"

"Go ahead and eat. Deadline's tomorrow, and this one's a doozie."

We exchanged I love you's and disconnected. Another agent called out a goodnight, I leaned forward, but the keyboard remained untouched, my byline the only words on the page. I eyed my bar cart.

This is a simplified example, but note the difference. In the first passage, the narrative tells the reader facts. In the second one, several of the same facts can be inferred: I live in New York. I am married to a man named Travis. I have more than one child. My husband is the primary caregiver. I write a column. This column is particularly challenging. It is after normal working hours. I don't like to "think without a drink." The first passage speaks to specifics, sure, but the second one gives you a scene with the same character and background but a more kinetic feel.

Thus, *telling* supplies information while *showing* explores information. In order to expand a narrative into more showing, think about the complete sensory experience of a scene (the sound of the "monkeys" in the background, the tone of the dialogue exchange, etc.). Obviously a certain amount of exposition is needed and wanted in order to establish the action portrayed, but when we veer too far into telling, we cater to the "info dump," which is a story-killer. Foie gras-ing the reader with information (yes, I am using *foie gras* as a verb, and who taught you to interrupt like that?) means you don't trust your own writing enough to allow the plot-essential details and facts to appear naturally in the execution. Don't fall into the trap of quickly getting pertinent information "out of the way" so you can "get to the story." You're better than that. Rather than reporting the facts, take your time to explore them through action, dialogue, and the senses of the characters involved.

And yes, I do have a bar cart in my office. It's always 11 A.M. *somewhere.*

Dear FYSA,

After reading my memoir, an agent told me that even though he "loved" the story, no major publishing house would touch it unless I had a substantial social media following. He said he'd reconsider representing me if I "could get social media moving." I am not a celebrity and have not been active on social media, but I believe I have a great story that would appeal to many. Won't I have a better chance of attracting followers once the book is published, rather than now?

Sincerely,
Cart Before Horse

Dear Lucy and the Football,

You said *Cart Before Horse*. But for me, it's Lucy and the Football. Charlie Brown knows what I'm talking about.

When I see a stunning memoir with zero platform attached—but, *Oh, that prose!* I laughed, I wept, I drank profusely (also known as: a Tuesday)—and I find myself talking about it over dinner, Husband always says, "You know you're going to end up doing it, so just do it." And then I run at it as hard as I can, and the author and I grind away for eighteen months trying to build that platform while hearing responses to our submissions along the lines of, "Still not enough platform," "Can you get Michelle Obama to blurb?" and, "This is great! Not with this guy, but if Aaron Rodgers were the author. ..." And then six months later a similar book comes out with Aaron Rodgers as the author. ... But wait, sweet victory, an offer! Only there's barely enough strength left in the author's hand to pick up the pen and sign the contract because *we left it all on the field.*

So it *can* be done, but it's a *lot* easier to get some media out there first.

Now, this doesn't mean you need to become Anderson Cooper. It just means you need to show growth and appeal within your targeted audience. And if your story is phenomenal, there isn't any reason why you shouldn't already be out there speaking to and publishing shorter pieces relating to the content of your memoir, anyway. Sites that are popular for their essays and opinion columns—think *Salon*, *Slate*, and *The Huffington Post*—and local media are great places to land bylines that will start organically growing social media platforms to discuss said content.

And if something you write should go viral? We agents will all come chasing you anyway, and so you'll kill all kinds of birds with that stone.

Here's my recommendation: Take six months and dedicate yourself to expanding your platform. See what you can shake loose.

Or, find a heart-on-her-sleeve sap like me to run at you so hard she gets bugs in her teeth. It's up to you.

Dear FYSA,

I would like to know how ghostwriters prove what they've worked on if they have signed confidentiality agreements. In your portfolio/ résumé, how would you prove that you in fact did ghostwrite that bestseller?

Sincerely,
Ghost(writer)

Dear Ghostie With the Mostie,

Hubba wha—? But … that's not a thing. *Is* this a thing? Hang on. …

[Flurry of confirmation calls to two agents, two editors, and a ghost.]

Okay, *phew.* I do know what I'm talking about. The "author" can't tell her ghostwriter, "You wrote this and now I have to kill you to silence you. And the editorial staff. And that guy in the weird pants who overheard me talking to you on my cell when I was in line at the bank that one time."

It is typical to be restricted from discussing a book's *content*, but atypical to be unable to refer to the work done *in certain specified instances.* At the point of negotiation of your ghost-writer's agreement, it should have been made clear as to what your "credit" will (or won't) be, and how any disclosure should be defined.

So I guess if this "and never the twain shall meet" is something you agreed to *under all circumstances* on a contractual level (you do have an agent or other legally versed professional advocating for you in signing major agreements, yes?), then, sorry, you have to stay zipped like a duck butt in a tsunami. But I have to say, I've done ghostwriter and co-writer deals from both sides of the table (including some that'd make you go, "Wait, *who* really wrote that?"), and they've all included a clause that allows the ghostwriter to confirm that he is indeed that mastermind behind the bestseller *should it pertain to securing other ghosting jobs*. Acknowledgment of your contribution should be specified up front, and can range from shared cover credit (whether "with" or "and") to an Acknowledgments page nod that doesn't define your role but is enough to confirm résumé status should the need arise. While nondisclosure agreements (NDAs) are as expected as they are necessary, no one should be out to ruin your chances of further employment.

Also, to anyone else considering ghostwriting, let me say from *vast* experience: If you do a bang-up job on a super-secret celebrity book, and you are all puppies and rainbows to work with, you won't need to figure out how to "reveal" anything ever again—as that publisher is going to chain you up in the basement and make you ghostwrite all its big stuff. And by *chain you up* I mean *pay you a kerbillion dollars*, and by *basement* I mean *mansion that you bought with your kerbillion dollars*. Your agent will have made her 15 percent of by creating an understanding in the contract that allows you to speak under the right circumstances as to how each one of those dollars was made.

Dear FYSA,

After yet another string of rejections that I've been told have nothing to do with the quality of my work ("Lovely, but I'm not the right editor," etc.) I feel really discouraged. I know we're always told that publishing is subjective, this comes with the territory, we must develop a thick skin, etc.—and usually I persevere. But something about this last experience has disillusioned me. I sit down at the keyboard and can't help feeling like, Why bother?

How do I move past this? I'm afraid you're going to say that the mere fact that I'm discouraged means I simply don't have what it takes to truly be a writer.

Sincerely,
On the Brink

Dear Brinksie,

Hand me that flask and scoot over. Because I hear you.

I have this client, we'll call her Michelle Gable (because that is her name), and I shopped several different manuscripts of hers for five years (What? Yes. Five. Years.) before I finally sold *A Paris Apartment*, which immediately became a national and international bestseller.

I can remember, after I think it was the third manuscript of hers that failed to sell, opening my office window and literally howling, "What is *wrong with you, Publishing?*" into the Manhattan wind. That was the first time I did that ... but not the last.

I wish I had a magical phrase to slur into your ear to make all of this easier, but I don't. I guess you and me? We need to remember that we do this because we *love* it, and because when we're *not* doing it we are cranky and mean and weird, and the highs are always higher than the lows are lower and that writers are a motley, stumbling, keening, glorious, brilliant, achingly beautiful community like no other and that sharing stories is part of our very humanity—it's what separates us from the dung beetles at least—and being part of the process of making that possible is humbling and awesome and quite simply the *Best. Thing. Ever.*

So, there's that.

Now stop bogarting the flask.

Dear FYSA,

My critique partner has just given me her novel—she is trying a new genre—and it is ... not good. Like, really not good. The characters seem trite and one-dimensional and the stakes are vapid and I almost couldn't even get through it. I really think this is a novel to set aside, but she really wants to show it to her agent. What is my responsibility here?

Signed,
Torn in Toluca Lake

Dear Torn,

Recently I was pulling some things out of a back closet to put in storage and I unzipped a garment bag and there was my wedding dress! I gasped and said to Husband, "Oh my gosh! It's still so pretty. I am going to try it on!" to which he blurted, "*Oh*, wow I don't know if *that's* a g—okay, yeah, of *course* you should," as I had already thrown off my T-shirt and sweat pants and started tugging it up my hips.

I yanked. I shimmied. I hopped. I stuffed. Then I scooted backward toward him and said, "Can you zip it?" and I felt a little pull as he did so and he said, "Okay, you're all set! Wow, you still look great in this, babe." I sashayed over to our full-length mirror and there she was. That blushing bride. Man, I loved that dress. I gazed for a moment at myself, then turned to the profile and noticed ... the dress didn't zip. And not like, didn't zip all the way up, but didn't zip at all. And there was an undulating mass of flesh preventing it from zipping. Like, ever again. I started grinning, then, I started laughing. Because *of course I don't fit in my wedding dress anymore!* But it was fun to try on and my goodness Husband showed a lot of grace in giving me the moment to enjoy without being like, "Yeah, why, you won't fit in that."

And that's what this moment is about—your critique partner knows this isn't her best foot forward. Especially if she has had success in other genres, she knows what her best writing feels like. She is trying this on and it is not a fit. And your role is to have grace. Try starting with, "Hey, Cathy, (even if her name isn't Cathy, go ahead and use it—I find this name to be soothing) I have been so spoiled previously by your work, and it has always felt so effortless—this feels a bit different. I have few questions, but can we first talk about the parts you feel need work so we can start there?" She'll let you know where the zipper feels stuck, and your job is to listen and support those feelings. In the end, she may still want to show this to her agent, and that's okay. When her agent comes back to her with the same concerns, you will have solidified your position as her trusted CP and next time neither of you will be torn. And that's good for CPs and dresses alike.

Dear FYSA,

A couple of my friends asked to read one of my stories, so I gave them copies. Neither of them ever mentioned it again. Should I assume they just got busy? Assume they hated it? Suck it up and ask? Forget about it? This is awkward.

Sincerely,
Afraid to Ask

Dear Afraid to Ask,

First of all, were they together when they asked? And so maybe when one guy asked, the other felt weird *not* asking, so piped up, "Oh yeah, me too"? If so, give 50 percent of them a pass. But, if this was more of a scattershot kind of thing, then on to my next question: Are they both self-described readers? If they're more likely to spend their time paging through *Golf Magazine* than reading stories in your genre, that can make a difference in both the impetus for asking and the response time.

Second—but wait, hang on, let me set down this toddler and this highball glass so I can gesture freely and wildly—*of course you should ask them what they thought!* Why wouldn't you?

Look. Nothing awkward here. Just ask. No one is going to be all, "Phil? I read it? And it was literally like that time in SoHo when that homeless guy stuck his finger in my mouth. I was as physically repulsed by your prose as when I could actually feel that man's fingernail graze my tongue."

If they truly are friends of yours, *and* if they did read it, they will probably say, "Oh yeah, it was pretty good! Are you working on something else?" And your job is then *not* to say something like, "But wait, did you get that any time the woman was wearing the blue scarf it was representing the dress her mother died in and therefore the overall unpredictable fragility of life?" Because you'll sound like a clown falling down a flight of stairs: just a series of desperate thumps and honks.

Here's the thing: A *huge* element in your writer's toolbox should be a critique partner or beta reader who you can depend on to give you an honest, constructive, and, yes, fairly prompt response. This should *not* be someone in your closest circle of family and friends. We have to see you a lot and therefore will probably lie a little.

Another important element is membership to a writing group, whether in person or online, where you are hearing from (and offering your own critiques in return to) others who may have a greater understanding of a missed note or troubled construct as well as an easier time using common language to discuss and suggest options on how to revise.

But for real, if you don't put this book down *right now* and text both of them, "Yo, I keep forgetting to ask: You read my thing yet?" you and I are *finished*.

Nah, we're good. But honestly, if you're nervous to hear what your friends think, how are you going to build up stamina when it comes time for an agent or editor to weigh in? Grab your loin-girding pants and get the feedback. Your work is counting on you.

Dear FYSA,

How far do you expect your authors to go with their research? Obviously if I am writing a thriller about a serial killer I am not going to go around killing people, but how do I keep the story authentic?

Sincerely,
Faking It

Dear Faker,

I support you in the "not killing" part, but you make a great point—thrillers are grounded in characters involved in high stakes and violence, so how does, say, an office supply store manager lend authenticity to a female cop protagonist? Or, more broadly, do you need to eat the cupcake to describe the cupcake?

Well, kind of.

I'd recommend that if anyone in your book is handling a gun you go to a gun range for a lesson with a certified instructor. Having fired a gun yourself will make a difference in how you describe those scenes. As an added bonus, a lot of folks who hang out at such places just happen to be former officers/armed forces/etc. and might be persuaded to tell a story or two from experience. Steal those.

You can also call police precincts, medical examiners, and county forensic labs and ask to have a brief fact check call with someone who can answer some procedural questions for you (though you may find that this is better received *after* you're published or under contract, just to confirm you're authentically researching and not a creeper). You might also try putting out a call on Facebook or Twitter: "Hey friends! Anybody got a relative in the police/armed forces that I can chat with to clarify some points in my book? I pay in beer and acknowledgments." People like to tell their stories. You'd be amazed at what you can find out if you just ask.

Dear FYSA,

I am writing a thriller and my agent keeps telling me to "pull back." But it's a thriller! *I'm concerned that she doesn't read enough in the genre to understand how fast-paced they are these days. But I also want her to love it enough to sell it. I know you sell a lot of thrillers—what do you think?*

Sincerely,
Less Than Thrilled

Dear Less Than Thrilled,

You know how freshly baked Subway sandwich bread *always* smells good? It wafts out into the street as you walk by, and no matter what you were thinking, the record in your head screeches and your brain interrupts to say, *Oh man, that smells amaaaazing.*

That's sort of the feeling I have when I hear, "I'm concerned she doesn't read enough in the genre to understand ..."—except when the record screeches, it smells less like Subway bread and more like decomposing goat corpse. I assume that this is an agent you chose due to the fact that she has thrillers on her list, and that you have had many a discussion about the genre you write in and the market for said genre—*right*? So what I'm more interested in addressing is the "pull back" comment that you don't agree with.

There are plenty of thrillers that amp things up to a certain level of pacing, content, and prose that will blow your hair back, [*Here's lookin' at you, Nick Petrie! Waves excitedly at Don Bentley!*], and there are others that still make your breath catch in your throat without leaving actual fingerprints on your neck [*Salutes Ren Richards!*] There is, however, a very fine line to tread between a cinematic thriller and an action movie that's poorly translated into print, and I can say I have seen a few manuscripts of late that have John McClane fist-fighting the jet plane *way* too often to keep the reader grounded.

Now, we can all point to great writers who top the bestseller lists with plot and pacing like they snorted rocket fuel, and when *you* top the list, you can do that too. But to really cement your initial contract with your debut readership, you are going to want to work very, very hard to keep things insanely taut, *yet accessible*. People don't want to read *action*; people don't want to read *thrills*. People want to read *characters committing to action* and *characters making decisions that lead to thrills* in the face of impossible obstacles, both internal and external. Hell, a man could just sit on a bench for an entire thriller if in the opening scene a bomb was wired to explode beneath that bench. Hold up. How badly do I want someone to write *that* book? [*Dials Sophie Littlefield.*]

Anyway, this is what I would have you consider: Have you created characters or *caricatures*? Are their decisions informing the plot, or is shit just blowing up? Make sure you are grounding the action in authentic and supported catalysts from three-dimensional characters, both the protagonist and the antagonist. Otherwise it's like that time I went to two *Sharktopus* showings in two different NYC bars, one at 9 P.M. and one at 1 A.M., and then woke up the next afternoon with mascara on my teeth and Cheetos in my hair: Sometimes too much of a good thing is just too much.

Dear FYSA,

I am the co-author of a 90-year-old man's story of his once-tumultuous life. Should we change the names of the persons who were responsible for his trauma? Even if we do, as long as the manuscript contains my co-author's real name, X and Y would easily identify themselves should they discover the book. Could we be held responsible for publishing negative information about their conduct?

Signed,
[Redacted]

Dear [Redacted],

The short answer: Yes. *Libel* (defaming a person in writing, as opposed to *slander*, which is damaging a person's character in speech) is something that an author can be sued over, and it can also be tough to defend when it's a matter of recollections that result in exposing the unsavory activities of a third party.

My client D. Watkins writes nonfiction and memoir and his debut *The Cook Up* (What? Oh yes, the INSTANT *New York Times* bestseller) outlines what happened when he took over the ... let's just call it "family business." That book is some of the most profound and evocative writing I've seen in my entire career, and definitely one of the books I am proudest of facilitating in its publishing journey. But his publisher had *plenty* of eyes on this manuscript in-house, *and* arranged for an outside legal vetting, to ensure that enough layers were in place to protect the innocent (and, well, the guilty). So, if there is any doubt that what you're writing is 100 percent factual, a legal professional would be your best resource in vetting the work in order to determine how closely the memoir treads the line of libel.

Dear FYSA,

Novels I've read by new authors lately—often, but not always, in the romance genre—seem to be really fast paced, with the characters having vivid sex, sometimes even before the end of the first chapter. Is that the new standard? I don't want my characters to seem cheap, but I also want to keep readers engaged. I guess what I'm wondering is: How much is too much?

Sincerely,
This Book Is Not Yet Rated

Dear Not Yet Rated,

How much is too much? First, let's pause for a beat here to allow my editor to slowly uncap her red pen with a look of utter terror …

Okay! So, actually, this is not the question you think it is. The fact of the matter remains that sex scenes, when done badly, are catastrophic to a novel. Therefore, it isn't about quantity, but *quality.* (Heh. That's [Editor: REDACTED].)

You should approach writing a sex scene the way you would approach describing a crime scene—because they both [Editor: REDACTED]. Am I right? Ha!

Think about it. The tension, the moment before, the gratuity level of the description, the atmosphere, and the construct of the characters involved are all integral to the crafting of a scene that works. You can begin a book with a crime as long as the moment is grounded in the *reality* of committing that crime, and not, *Guy enters, shoots, exits.* The same goes for a sex scene in an opening chapter. I mean, because [Editor: REDACTED—*this is getting exhausting.*]

Look, when writing plots peppered with the biggies—death, sex, fear, and love—the most important factor is how relatable the motivations of the characters are. *That* is what the plot revolves around. People don't want to read about actions; they want to read about people making decisions that *lead* to those actions. Trying to write a scene that feels inorganic to the established construct of the character (regardless, by the way, of whether or not the character is likeable), isn't going to do readers any favors—whether the character is having sex or making an omelet.

And, heh, in both cases, [Editor: REDACTED].

Dear FYSA,

I've heard that including chapter titles in novels is passe and the sign of an amateur. What are your thoughts?

Yours,
Passe the Potatoes

Dear Passe,

Chapter 1: What If That *Is* What It's All About?

It was 1983. Brett, that mulleted roller god, had just circled the Great Skate patrons for the prize round of "The Hokey Pokey." The music started. I put my right hand in. The rest should have been history. But no! As we put our whole selves in, he skated over, feathered bangs ruffling in the self-made breeze, and handed the jumbo pink bear to the girl *next* to me. To this day I am boggled, incensed, inflamed by this travesty of justice. I hokied! I pokied! *She didn't even turn herself around.*

Now *that* is an amateur.

Hmm? Oh. You're still here. Chapter titles? It's fine to use them as long as they enhance rather than distract.

Dear FYSA,

I have an idea for a young adult book regarding concussions—but when I mentioned it to my fiction workshop teacher, he said it wouldn't be worth my time. Still, I'd really like to write this book. Could I get your expert opinion on its viability?

Signed,
Eager Survivor

Dear Survivor,

While this question might at first glance seem a bit narrow to address for a wide audience, I want anyone who has ever had an idea shot down by a supposed authority to take heed.

I have to say, my gast is totally flabbered that anyone would dissuade a student from pursuing something based on an idea alone … unless it was as blatantly off the mark as, say, revamping *50 Shades of Grey* for a middle-grade audience.

Among the things I bark at my clients through my headset while jabbing my finger in the air (e.g. "No! You 'taking a break to eat' means my bank account takes a break from money!" or, "Sleep is for second place!") is "Obey the muse!" These authors' creative impulses behave much the way my children do: I can try to guide them, but I certainly cannot control them.

In truth, I've been known to bring the hammer down on an idea that waves a red flag, but only *after* I see actual pages to understand how the idea is explored. Among those flags might be:

- a narrative depicting a member of a marginalized group in an inorganic or insensitive way;
- a narrative that is so familiar to its genre that it covers no new ground;
- gratuitous and/or inorganic scenes of violence or sex.

This is also why I personally tend to prefer sample chapters to pitch sessions: *Talking* about an idea is never an author's best representation of how he will explore that topic. On the surface, some ideas are indeed better than others, but unless this idea was offered among potential story trajectories that shone brighter, I would not dissuade you from pursuing it. (Also, grab your teacher a copy of my client Eileen Cook's YA book *With Malice*, and I think you may be able to demonstrate that comparative titles for this theme do in fact exist.)

Dear FYSA,

My novel received a couple of rejections with recurring comments about it being "too quiet." That was my intent, though. I want the book to feel like an afternoon at the park, not like a fistfight. Am I just soliciting the wrong people for my type of story, or do I really need to add more drama and conflict to make it publishable?

Yours,
Peaceful Pam

Dear Peaceful,

Okay, not to completely expose how wildly I leveled up in my life-partner choice, but this one time I only agreed to go to the MOMA if Husband would agree to take me to see *Live Free or Die Hard* that night.

Reader, he married it.

But explosions and Bruce Willis beating up a fighter plane are not necessarily the kinds of drama and conflict your novel needs in order to avoid the "quiet" label. What that generally speaks to are the stakes involved for the characters moving through the story. There should be a resonance from the reader to the characters, a subconscious identification with the conflict pushing against the protagonist getting what she wants. If it is too esoteric or doesn't have a large enough impact on the character arc, beautiful writing won't be enough to keep the narrative's neck above still waters.

But also, to totally contradict everything I just said: Sometimes quiet *is* okay! We've all read books that were deeply satisfying because they felt like a canoe trip on a glass-surfaced lake during a languid sunset. There is space for quiet on the shelves ... but it would be misleading if I didn't admit that it's a narrower space than the book that marries higher-stakes conflict with accessible prose.

Dear FYSA,

Agents' submission guidelines routinely categorize fiction submissions as "commercial," "upmarket," and "mainstream." Can you explain the differences? I'd also find it helpful to have an example of a successfully published author or book from each.

Sincerely,
Category Curious

Dear Curious,

Pinpointing the genre is a fundamental aspect of being able to talk about your book, but the lines here can be a bit slippery, like shades on a color wheel blended into a murky goulash.

First, let me clarify: You asked about three categories, but I don't usually use the term *mainstream*. Maybe I'm splitting hairs, but in these broad terms I think *mainstream* and *commercial* are interchangeable (though mainstream *can* refer to commercial fiction that doesn't fit neatly into a popular genre). The three overarching categories my agency uses to describe and pitch novels are generally *commercial*, *upmarket*, and *literary*.

COMMERCIAL FICTION is the hot fudge sundae on the menu: a slam-dunk satisfier for the widest of audiences. You'll find delightful variations—sprinkles or nuts, mystery or romance—but overall you can feel comfortable recommending it to someone else who likes desserts, because they will likely find it accessible and satisfying.

UPMARKET FICTION is more like tiramisu. There are folks who enjoy it, and some who don't. The palate may need to be a little more refined to appreciate it, and maybe you'll be dressed a little fancier when you order it, yet it's still a relatively accessible dessert with satisfying but identifiable components—albeit presented in a more original way.

LITERARY FICTION is green tea chocolate mousse with a raspberry reduction. Some folks will think, "Yeah, no, that just sounds like a bunch of trying too hard." Others will be attracted to the lushness of it all—and this target group is looking to be satisfied by a unique construct.

Let's look at this question another way: Different sets of readers have certain expectations about how a book is going to get them from "It was a dark and stormy night" to "And they lived happily ever after." Whether the ride is turbulent or smooth, first class or coach, a lead aspect in each of these categories is up front in the cockpit, keeping us on track to land. So, let's see who is flying the plane:

Commercial Fiction: The plot flies the plane.
Upmarket Fiction: The characters fly the plane.
Literary Fiction: The prose flies the plane.
This is getting fun. Let's do it in haiku!

Commercial fiction
Entices broad audience
Nicholas Sparks, yo.

Upmarket fiction
With wine and cheese at Book Club
Jodi Picoult, friend.

Literary Fic
Lush and meaty craft throughout
What up, Donna Tartt?

Dear FYSA

If my latest story idea is similar to a published novel, should I bother to write it? The existing book is fantasy, is moderately popular but not famously so, and there are distinct differences between the two.

Sincerely,
Notta Copycat

Dear Notta,

A little side-smirk phrase we use in publishing is "the same, but different" when talking about what we're pitching/selling. That's because in the aggressively competitive entertainment world, we aren't just competing with other books, but other media, media that we can hold in our hand: YouTube, Netflix, HBOGo, Amazon Prime, Hulu (not to mention then losing an additional two hours feeling teeth chattering envy of our friends' lives as depicted on social media).

The average person has a finite amount of dollars allocated for entertainment, so if they've read and loved something, they're more likely to be willing to dish out the Benjamins for something *guaranteed* to be worth the time and money spent. That's why you see stuff like *Gone Girl* followed by every other *Girl* title in every other incarnation you can imagine. We're hoping to snatch that audience away from their Twittergrams and Instafeeds and say, "Dude, remember that book you *totally loved*?! This is like that, *the same but different*, so you are *totally* gonna love this one too!" My clients, Alexandra Villasante and James Brandon both write books which focus on and explore young adult narratives with marginalized protagonists and often tour and appear on panels together because there is cross over audience there—but their books themselves could not be more different albeit they are under the same broad umbrella.

And let's be honest: Ever since that time a million years ago around the campfire when our good buddy Grok grunted out, "Folks love. Bad stuff happens. Folks figure it out okay," there haven't been that many new stories to tell—just new ways to tell them. Whoa. I literally started applying Grok's synopsis to the last three books I read, and it holds up. Try it.

See?

Dear FYSA,

I've already been over my manuscript once and believe it's a strong first draft. My next step is to get developmental notes from an independent editor and make revisions according to her critique, then start submitting to agents. Because so many agents are hands-on with editing, is it fair to assume that two advance revisions on my part are enough—and then I'll comply with any additional suggestions from the agent?

Yours,
Reggie Rewriter

Dear Reggie,

Your question is interesting because the process you've described here to establish "readiness" is more *quantitative* than *qualitative*, and that isn't exactly the right tool of measurement.

Instead, let's approach this from a more qualitative view, and with that in mind *sing it with me*: **Consider a critique partner (or two)!** It can also be helpful to get someone who isn't *paid* by you to weigh in on the story's cohesiveness and submission readiness, especially if a gentle but firm "This isn't going to get there. Time to shelf it and shake loose something new" is needed.

More important, you don't want your manuscript to go out if you have *any* inclination that further revisions are needed. These days the landscape is so wildly competitive that you want your book to be in the best shape possible. Yes, an agent will provide further editorial guidance, as will an editor, of course, but both of those pros are looking for work that is already as close as possible to publication-ready. There is no reason to send anything out *knowing* it still needs work, as you're just putting more obstacles in your path.

Seek out readers who can give you further confirmation that you have something that is *truly* in the best shape you can get it before presenting it to the next level.

Dear FYSA,

Is it bad for your career to try writing in a completely different genre if you don't have any luck getting an agent with the genre you've been focused on?

Sincerely,
Genre Roulette

Dear Roulette,

Look, if you'd *like* to try a different genre, I absolutely support that. But only in the event that you feel creatively driven to do so, and *not* if you're switching gears because you think it might be a better way to get an agent or to get published or to *get* anything.

The latter assumption *is* bad for your career, much like saying, "Well, this juggling thing didn't work out—guess I'll hop on a unicycle!" It might be the same circus, but it's an entirely different skill set.

I often field a similar question from folks who've been trying to write for adults and think, *Well,* this *isn't working, so maybe I'll just write a young adult novel instead.* There is an egregiously incorrect assumption in some circles that writing for teens or middle-graders is easier than writing for adults. Take it from me: It's not.

I have also heard some casual commenting along the lines of, "You know, if I wrote *commercial* fiction, I could have had an agent yesterday." *Commercial fiction* isn't code for *easier to write* fiction, and you just made the rest of us want to talk about you behind your back for saying that. (In fact, we're going to, and we're going to eat pie while we do it.)

Chasing some idea about what sells or what agents want isn't going to be the best path toward publication. If you have a backlist of previous manuscripts spanning historical fiction, fantasy, YA, upmarket fiction, and memoir—all with no takers—that's more likely a sign that you need to devote more attention to improving your craft and less attention to following perceived industry trends.

If you *still* feel pulled to make a switch, I hope it's because you have read several dozen books across that genre and then one day your muse showed up with a book premise, a bouquet of flowers, and a handwritten note that says, "I'm just going to keep whispering this idea until you open a blank document and start typing." *Those* are the right reasons.

When you're done, you and your muse are welcome to stop over for some pie.

Dear FYSA,

I'm an older male writer, and when I look at books on the shelves in stores, or what agents are seeking, almost everything seems geared toward the female or young adult readers: romances with bare-chested males or cottage mysteries about cooking. I've written in just about every genre except those, and have no desire to start. Am I putting myself at a disadvantage by not writing for a more popular readership? Since this is all publishers seem to be putting out, are they the only titles that are selling? I'll keep writing, but right now I see no path to success.

Yours,
Jaded Joe

Dear Jaded Joe,

Hmmm ... what shelves are you looking at? Thrillers, mysteries, and crime novels are still male dominated insofar as sales numbers, and while names like King, Koontz, Patterson, Grisham, and Thor roll off the tongue, I challenge you to immediately name five female authors in that same genre. I am wondering if perhaps the "path to success" might be paved with visiting other bookstores.

Maybe what *is* penetrating right now is the industry-wide intention to get more diversity on the shelves, both with authors and characters, which isn't intended to be exclusionary and is still vastly outweighed by the majority of published authors being white males.

Regardless, try chatting with your local librarian and booksellers about who is coming off the shelves the fastest these days. Conversations are free, and you might find yourself picking up a new title and giving it a try.

Dear FYSA,

I have a couple of legal questions: First, should I copyright my manuscript before submitting to agents? And second, I'm writing fiction but I reference a real product and celebrity. Will I get sued?

Sincerely,
Leery of Litigation

Dear Leery,

If you file for a copyright number with the U.S. Copyright Office before your book is published, then you've registered the wrong version of the book. Unless you plan on having *zero* revisions. And even when I'm 100-percent certain that my client is a genius, they *always* have many, many more than zero revisions. The final version of your manuscript is what needs to be registered, and that will be handled between you and the publisher as outlined in your contract. So, in summation: *Nope* on the copyright. Besides, if you're worried about folks stealing your ideas, your title, your character, it's very difficult to prove an idea has been stolen unless entire sections have been copied verbatim.

As far as your libel concerns: Yeah, anyone can sue anyone at any time for anything they deem to be libelous. If there are legitimate concerns, I might caution you to ask yourself a question regarding the object and person of concern: Is the opinion or view of the object central to the plot?

A character can call his Toyota Corolla a piece of garbage if it's the reason a robbery went south. But you might be tempting fate to have that character announce that *all* Toyota Corollas are pieces of garbage.

Does the character clearly represent a real-life person, and does their portrayal come from a personal desire to watch said person suffer upon publication?

Celebrities have a much higher threshold for any kind of libel claim—with fame, one seems to waive some protection in the public arena. But what you cannot do is put a thinly veiled version of your ex-wife in the book and call her a smut-peddling petri dish who kicks puppies for fun. Your ex-wife is not a public figure and therefore the standard for libel is *much* lower—and the chuckles you may get while writing her "character" will quickly turn to tears when her lawyer calls. Quality writers know that words have power, and they respect that. Using your novel for petty get-backsies or celebrity bashing is beneath all of us.

Dear FYSA,

I've written a manuscript that has been rejected by fifty or so agents, many of whom have said that while they like the writing style, they felt like the genre (which I've tried labeling as "upmarket speculative" and "dystopian satire" in queries) is too nebulous or in-between to attract a publisher. Is a book from a debut author without a clear section on bookshelves too much of a gamble for agents?

Sincerely,
Adrift in Anaheim

Dear Adrift,

I sat with this question awhile. Part of my response would entail me standing with you in the rain outside of some sort of Irish drinking establishment, shaking our fists and howling, "But it worked for Moore! It worked for Palahniuk and Adams! *What's the problem here?*" And another part would be me wearing a fitted suit, drinking from a mug that says "World's Okayest Mom," looking up over my glasses and saying, "Then write something else," and doing a dismissive hand-flicky thing.

All I can say is this: If you've heard back from fifty agents, you're crushing it. Even if they're all rejections, you're doing full due diligence to serve your novel from soup to nuts. But there is *something* about it that prevents an agent from seeing the path. Because, no, *nothing* is too much of a gamble if I truly love it. I will go out with a novel that has a talking dog on skis that fights zombies if I feel like I will forever regret not being a part of this book that I think brings magic to the table. But in this case, you have *fifty agents* that would clearly see another query from you, if not request the full. Because it isn't your craft or skill level in question here, and that right there is an answer. It may not be the answer you wanted, but look at it like this: fifty folks in publishing just said you got the writing chops. So find the plot that respects that … Hey, Sparky! Here boy! Strap on your skis!

Dear FYSA,

I've been getting a few rejections on my novel saying things like, "The narrative didn't resonate," and, "I couldn't connect with the execution." What does that really mean?

Signed,
Don't Mince in Milwaukee

Dear Don't Mince,

First, if you are getting anything beyond a form rejection—which you are, as agents or editors have taken time to point out a resonance issue—then you are just riding the subjectivity horse into the next town. Keep querying! This sometimes simply means that one man's *Colour Me Good Benedict Cumberbatch* is another man's *The Goldfinch*.

But there *could* also be a structural issue, a content/style issue or both. Here are three of the most common issues I find in manuscripts where the narrative fails to resonate:

1. **CHARACTERS ASKING THEMSELVES QUESTIONS:** Readers can feel a disconnect when writers overuse this device to establish how the reader should perceive the scene at hand.

   Let me introduce a mantra: *Keep the narrative declarative*. Scrap the questions in the protagonist's head, and let the reader ask them instead.

2. **AN OVERABUNDANCE OF DEMONSTRATIVE ADJECTIVES:** Think of demonstrative adjectives as linguistic signposts that indicate which noun the writer is referring to. Too many can muddy the clarity of what you're trying to get across. For instance, compare these two statements:

   > Barbara picked up the Benedict Cumberbatch coloring book that was on the table that was given to her by her grandmother.

   > Barbara picked up the Benedict Cumberbatch coloring book her grandmother gave her from the table.

3. **PACING ARM-WRESTLING PROSE:** When an author can't quite find the balance between prose and pacing, it's tough for me to overlook. Even with gorgeous phrasing, when the writing actually gets in the way of the … well … *writing*, it's like listening to Mozart while standing next to a seal with influenza—just an unpredictable blast of dissonance that makes the reader experience unstable.

   > Barbara, a lugubrious, unintelligible bay building in volume and mournfulness keening between her lips, placed her sparsely jeweled right hand against her chest, feeling the timapnic lub-

> dub of her aorta, as her wretched discovery took hold: there would be no Benedict today.
>
> Barbara was irritated and sad.

Again, these are just the three issues I most commonly can *define* when I am not connecting with a manuscript. For the most part, however, when I personally say that a manuscript didn't resonate with me, it is just simply a nebulous statement that meant I was able to put it down and not pick it up again. Which isn't a sign that you should quit—just that you should keep looking for the right agent match.

Dear FYSA,

I hear all kinds of little bon mots in my writer's group, but the repeated ones are always "write drunk, edit sober" and "write what you know." What are your thoughts on the validity of those quips?

Yours,
Catching Phrases

Dear Catch,

If you're new here, you might be unaware that from time to time I sling around spirits—both in my prose and all over the keyboard. But truthfully, I feel that writing under *any* influence does more to hamper the creative process than enhance it. I have a client who took more than three years to complete revisions on a glorious book, then got sober and wrote his next book—a wild ride of a thriller—in less than six months. His explanation: "Things went a lot faster when I wasn't squinting through one eye to see the screen."

That's not to say you can't have a glass of pinot keyboard-side while you clack away, but I think the kind of synapses that are firing when one is *three* glasses in are just creating more work for the next day's editorial process. I say write and edit sober. Leave the drinking for celebrating on days when you pump out 2,000 words, or for your kids' tap dance recitals.

As far as "write what you know" … like, if you are a cis-gender, married white woman with two children, and a penchant for telling others to drink less while you spill Tito's on your keyboard, do I think that's the only lens through which you should be writing? Not at all. Just be *aware* and *authentic* in your portrayals, prose, and plotting, do your research, and you can anchor us in the emotion of the story—the ache and need and loss and elation and pain and terror and love and hope. We all "know" those.

PART 2

Finding and Working With an Agent

I love it when I am at a writers' event, and someone raises their hand and asks with a smirk "Why do I even *need* an agent?" I always say, "Ya don't!" And move on to another question. Because, ya don't. You can self-publish! You can work with a small press and do the negotiation yourself! You can work with a large press and do the negotiation yourself! You can choose whatever path feels the best for you and your career. Kinda like deciding to use a real estate broker or to sell by owner. There are pros and cons on both sides. And what the public sees as far as "what an agent does" is oftentimes just the final tie-breaking kick through the uprights, not the blood, sweat, and tears it took to get to the field in the first place.

It is important, however, to make sure the agent you sign with is the right one for you—and you will have ample time to ask that agent questions before you sign. I have included a list of suggested questions in the back of the book as a guide for when you get that thrilling call—because when the moment comes, you will forget everything you wanted to ask and do some blurting which you then will verbally berate yourself over when you hang up. See? I am already agenting you behind the scenes, keeping you informed and secure and focused.

Agents may never get their Steve Gleason moment. You'll never *see* us block that kick. But we're there, diving, arms outstretched clearing the path for your big score.

So go forth! Find your agent. Because now? Now the real work begins.

Dear FYSA,

In today's market, with print-on-demand, e-books, and inexpensive publishing routes, do I even need to consider having a literary agent? Are agents still relevant?

Signed,
Dancing Solo

Dear Solo,

Interestingly I have never had a client ask that question.

And *need* is just such a funny word to me. Because actually, what do we all need really besides food, water, shelter, and vodka? And some peep toe wedges. And reruns of *Murder She Wrote.*

But I digress.

So! Do you *need* an agent? Look, I don't *need* Spanx. But I know that when I have them, they are taking care of my business. I get the support and the overall confidence to perform at my best and focus on what I need to accomplish without worry. If my Spanx could also enrich my talent, exponentially increase my income, sell to major New York publishers, sell to foreign territories, secure me a film option, and have any career-related conversation on my behalf that frankly I just didn't want to have, sounds like I am going to have a much smoother go of it.

But in the end, if you do not feel an agent is necessary for your desired career path, that gets to be okay, too! You have to establish what your journey is going to look like on your terms, and if it is one without a partner, I certainly wouldn't begrudge you that. And I will say this: A bad agent is *way* worse than no agent. Off-brand Spanx don't do anyone any favors.

Dear FYSA,

My sixteen-year-old daughter aspires to become a professional literary agent. How does one get into the field?

Yours,
Future Focused

Dear Focused,

This question has an answer as varied and nuanced as each of our industry's agents. Some folks get on track as an English major undergrad, some by going to law school. Others start in an entirely different track and then hop trains to a program like the Columbia Publishing Course. There are summer internships, mailroom positions, friends of friends who hear about an open entry-level assistant position.

There are also those who think to themselves, *Hey! I love to read and I really love my own opinions.* So they charm and cajole—some might say *hound*—an amazing literary agent until she finally calls while they're on a run in Central Park and says, "You just won't seem to go away, will you? That alone means something to your potential. Do you want the job?" And then, *Pow!* You're an agent!

Okay, okay, maybe not that last one. That seems too crazy to be true. [*Side eye.*]

The most ubiquitous trait you can find in an agent, however, is the story they tell when asked, "Why books?" Sometimes books helped to escape; sometimes they helped to stay grounded. Sometimes books were an only friend, or they were the only friends you wanted. Sometimes you saw yourself in a book, sometimes you saw someone else in one. Sometimes they provided the laugh you didn't know you needed. Sometimes they provoked the cry you knew you did. Because you have to *love* these delicious, wondrous, marvelous things—these books. The baseline for any agent is *the love of the story.*

I believe similar characteristics extend to editors—those invaluable muses, those keepers of the craft—and that might be another path for your daughter to investigate. As an editor, you are still working with words and helping to shape art and education (disguised as entertainment—*whee!*). And not to put too fine a point on it, because I am usually very, *very* subtle, but editors receive a salary. Agents work on commission: We get paid when we sell a book. Basically, we only eat what we kill, and there can be some mighty feasts, but also some terrible famines.

Wanna see the math? Let's say that on Day 1, an agent sells a book to Putnam for $100,000. *Wowie!* A six-figure deal! But before you order the caviar, let's unpack that number a bit. The agent takes 15 percent, which in this make-believe scenario comes out to $15,000. As part of an agency, the starting rate for an agent is usually half of that 15 percent—meaning the agent takes home $7,500. But that $7,500 is often paid out in *halves* (or smaller fractions). One half on contract signing, the other half on Delivery and Acceptance (D&A) of the client manuscript. So that is $3,750 up front, and the other $3,750 around *six months later.*

Before taxes.

So, less caviar, more ... fish sticks.

This peek behind the curtain is not meant to discourage, only to reveal one of the many aspects that differentiate the editorial side of publishing from the agenting side, and *both* are very worthy, very fulfilling avenues to keep books as your passion *and* your vocation. I'm just saying, it might make sense for your daughter to keep her mind open. But at age sixteen, the most important education/preparation she could have—before taking a class, enrolling in a publishing course or targeting a Master of Fine Arts program—is to read, read, read. Everything. Tell your daughter to think of the books she devours in the context of what else is out on the shelves, making comparisons like, "That book is *The Devil Wears Prada* meets *The Martian*." (Okay, whatever *that* book is, I really need it.) And make sure she's able to substantiate it. Encourage her to enter into discussions with others about what they are reading, and to facilitate a genuine interest in *why* they're reading it.

And if she's *still* set on the agenting side? Tell her to start to … challenge norms. But with *flair*! I mean obviously not *your* norms. Rules are rules! (*Psst* … hey, kid … you want half an hour added to your curfew? Ask for an hour, get the "No," counter with forty-five minutes and a check-in call. They'll settle at that extra thirty. *Boom*.) Being an agent is about finding the path that leads to everyone standing up from the table feeling that their needs were met—and that is achieved through persistence and, quite frankly, panache. So, she needs to read and persevere. Then, who knows? Maybe your daughter will be jogging in Central Park one day and I'll give her a call.

I hear that's a thing.

Dear FYSA,

It's my understanding that, broadly speaking, agents help authors in two ways: 1.) They find a publisher, and 2.) They negotiate the terms of publication. For this, they receive 15 percent commission. My question is this: If the author finds a publisher on her own and then approaches an agent for representation, is it appropriate to ask the agent to accept less?

Sincerely,
Commission Quandary

Dear Commissioner,

Why not? Technically, the Association of Authors Representatives (the accrediting agency for our profession) lets agents charge whatever they want to. Some agents even adjust their commissions for reprints or foreign editions. And hey, you can't hear *yes* if you never ask, right?

Oh, but you're going to hear *no*. You should, anyway, if the agent is worth her salt. In black and white, yes: The agent finds a publisher, negotiates a contract, then is the liaison for the life of the contract in the publication process. But that's kind of like saying a spouse 1.) buys you a ring, and then 2.) hangs out with you until you're dead.

In the rainbow of color that is the *rest* of the agent's job description, you will also find: manager, confidant, psychoanalyst, assistant researcher, cheerleader, conductor, taskmaster, advocate, kitten, pit bull, squeaky wheel, sales associate, Nosferatu, publicist, great white shark, cookie-cutter shark, enforcer, instigator, peacemaker, fortune teller, business partner, and perhaps even friend—with any luck, for the next thirty years or so.

Indeed, it is a tough relationship to describe to anyone who hasn't had a (good) agent, and suggesting that the only things an agent provides can be broken down into your original two columns devalues the overall business arrangement and may start the union off on a crooked foot. I would suggest instead that you focus on what the agent can bring to the lead you already have. For example, just in the very first conversation you can inquire about: better contractual terms, further submission opportunities, long-term career vision, short-term career vision, foreign marketability and sales, film marketability and sales, audio marketability and sales, and the list goes on. If the agent is able to constructively answer, it should provide you with a slice of insight into how much she can assist and therefore *earn* that 15 percent. If she says immediately that she is fine with 10 percent, I question instead whether that is the right agent for you as she would arguably be able to reconcile giving you only two-thirds of her services and attention.

Dear FYSA,

I'm a ghostwriter/ghost editor (nonfiction only). Is there anything wrong with my sending queries to agents on behalf of a client? Most clients, though experts in their fields, are neophytes when it comes to publishing and have no idea how to proceed. Would a query from a professional writer (from their "developmental editor" for instance) help them? Or does the agent want to see the query come directly from the client?

Sincerely,
Behind the Scenes

Dear Behind the Scenes,

Back in the late 90s, I was set up on a blind date—and by *blind*, I mean that this was back when you couldn't even e-snoop, and so I had zero interaction with the fella. Before I met the guy in person, our mutual friend did all the talking, extolling his virtues, raving about his "George Clooney looks" and how funny he was.

Well, let's just say that our virtuous George did make a pun or two, but I think his casual racism *riiiiiiight* before the appetizers was maybe what stuck out the most for me on *that* particular date.

We could have spared each other more than a tank of gas if we would have connected person-to-person first without the middleman attempting to sell us on the union.

If a person is ill-informed as to how to conduct themselves on step *one* of the publishing path, that doesn't bode well for the journey. Rather than giving these people a can of tuna, hand them a rod and reel and direct them to the nearest fishing hole. There are many, many books and guides on how to write a query (and an Internet search might even turn up a Writer's Digest webinar or two that I have taught on the subject).

Look, queries ain't brain surgery. I advise writers to break them down into three paragraphs using a little rhyme scheme I have "borrowed" (as in, I heard it at a conference years ago and can't remember who said it):

- **THE HOOK:** An intro including log line, word count, and genre (including any comp titles: "This is ____meets ____").
- **THE BOOK:** Four to five sentences explaining the premise.
- **THE COOK:** A bit about the author. Basically: Why this book, why me, why now.

Voilà! Queried.

Of course, nonfiction clients will also need a book proposal, for which there are also myriad resources. You can offer your clients an extra set of eyes on their submissions materials to point out weaknesses or bolster the feel, but I want the query from the author to be their authentic effort. That way even if it has mistakes, we are coming from an organic first step.

Dear FYSA,

I'm having a hard time making my synopsis brief enough to conform with agent guidelines. How can I determine what really needs to be in it and what I can leave out?

Sincerely,
Summary Stumped

Dear Stumped,

I have a dear friend who describes movies in such detail that by the time she's done, I'm surprised to find I'm not holding popcorn and gummy bears. This is a double-edged sword, however, as sometimes I just want to ask, "What's it about?" and have her say, "A tsunami drops super crocs on a small bayou town," because that is all I need to hear to know that I am *in*.

Generally speaking, you should have the ability to describe your novel in three different ways:

1. THE LOG LINE: This is a one-sentence refined summary that boils the work down to its broadest definition. This can sometimes use the formula of "[well-known book] meets [well-known book]," but regardless of what form it takes, it should reveal both the genre and conflict within a single line: "Great white shark terrorizes small New England beach town."

Now, being familiar with Peter Benchley's *Jaws*, among the best things about that novel are the characterizations and the relationships between Brody, Hooper, and Quint. But that isn't necessary to get into with a log line. We just illuminated the listener to both the genre and the conflict in fewer than ten words.

2. THE ELEVATOR PITCH: This consists of five to six lines that expand on the log line to summarize your novel, should you ever be in an elevator with me (and I usually soft-shoe in elevators, so you'll want to put a stop to that any way you can). This is also handy so that when you tell people you're a novelist at parties and they ask what your book is about, you can tell them without their eyes glazing over. You want to make sure you are capturing the genre and the conflict, as you do in the log line, but you can expand a bit more on the main character(s).

So, this is where you get a little meatier (but not indulgent):

> A great white shark terrorizes a small New England beach resort town over Fourth of July weekend. The sheriff is met with resistance by the mayor and the local business owners when he tries to close the beaches. But when swimmers are being systemically devoured, the sheriff, a marine biologist, and a salty old sea dog go on the hunt of their lives knowing that out in open water, they are not the top of the food chain.

3. THE SINGLE-PAGE SUMMARY: This is generally what agents look for when they request a synopsis. It should be three to five paragraphs, and get into more about the characters and their conflicts. This is where you would outline that the sheriff is a family man struggling against a town that simply doesn't believe there is a threat. Then we unfold the plot and introduce Hooper and Quint with a couple of lines about their backstories, and then we're goin' on a shark hunt and *voilà*! A synopsis.

Note: A synopsis is not a detailed pitch, like a long version of your query, but a true summary. Thus it should explain the full story arc, sometimes even including the ending. Even though you might think the twist that will "really get me" is now "ruined," the reasoning here is actually in your favor: If there is something nagging at me in the execution of your opening chapters, but I then read your synopsis and find out there's a spectacular ending worth the ride, I'll be more inclined to work with you on revisions.

If you ever feel like you want to tell more than what agents appear to need to hear, it usually means you want to make sure we understand the uniqueness of the construct of either your plot or your characters. And we will! The writing will show that, not the synopsis. Just try to introduce your work the way you would set me up on a blind date—tell enough to make it clear why I should be interested and why this is a good match, but don't go into too many details about all the players involved. Just get us in the boat.

Dear FYSA,

Today as I was doing some job searching online in the library, some guy in a messy, beat-up jacket came up to me and said he's a literary agent and he's interested in finding a publisher for my novel. I was flattered, because he complimented me on my natural red hair and he noticed I was a college graduate, which got us to the conversation of how I'm becoming a writer.

Bottom line: He wants to look at my novel and shop it to publishers. But since he wasn't dressed professionally and he looked like he didn't shower, my instincts are telling me not to trust him. I've asked for his credentials through my professional Facebook account and he hasn't responded yet because it got sent to his "Other" folder. What should I do?

Sincerely,
Miss Red Flag

Dear Miss Red Flag,

He sounds *awesome*. If he also asked to borrow a few bucks then I wouldn't say sign with him—I would say *marry* him!

Well, no. Okay. It's kind of obvious here that this isn't your advocate, but not for the reasons you might think.

I mean, just take the unshowered look: Literally this very morning as the clock ticked jackrabbit fast toward eight, *something* had to give, by God. So, I shaved my legs in the bathroom sink with half a slice of toast hanging out of my mouth, and barked at my children to "make their own lunches" which I now know will consist of Skittles poured into a Crown Royal bag. Then I came into the office, noticed I had a sock somehow lodged into the sleeve of my shirt and closed a multi-book deal for an author.

You might catch me on an off-shower day, but that doesn't mean I'm not cranking it out for ya.

But indeed, let's talk a bit about the common red flags used to identify the differences between Agent and Schmagent:

READING FEES: Agents only get paid when *you* get paid. Shmagents might reference a "reading fee." No legit agent will ask for a reading fee. Ever, at any point. We get paid when you get paid. Period.

MEDIA PRESENCE: Most agents have a website or at least a page on Facebook or Publishers Marketplace detailing clients and sales. Schmagents might ask you to reach out to them through their social media accounts, not an official website or query in box.

SUBMISSION PLAN SPECIFICS: An agent should be able to tell you which imprints—and sometimes even specific editors—she is considering sending the book to, and why. Not just "HarperCollins." Schamgents might even have solicited an editor on a social media forum in public.

ONLINE CHATTER: Sites such as QueryTracker and Agent Query chronicle writers' experiences, good and bad, to help you determine the reputability of an agent. Schmagents might have negative reviews on one or more of these sites.

REFERENCES: An agent should connect you to another client(s) as a reference if requested. Shmagents will give you limited folks to connect with or talk around you connecting with them at all.

And yes, I have also approached writers in the wild. *But*, there are things writers need to be wary of when this sort of thing happens.

WHEN ENCOUNTERED IN THE WILD:

An Agent will:

- Ask what genre you write in.

- Inquire about log line/elevator pitch
- Ask how many words you have/what draft stage you are in.
- Mayyyybe hand you a card and say, "Send me a query and a couple of chapters when you're done—you never know, right?" and leave it at that.

A Schmagent will:

- Offer to represent your manuscript before reading it.
- Say things like "look at your novel and shop it to publishers."
- Make grand promises regarding an auction or a huge advance, or a timeline in which your work will "for sure sell." (This is not a primary identifying trademark of a Schmagent, however, as I have mouthed off in similar fashion … the difference being, *I was right*. HEY GURRRRRL! *toasts with coffee cup* *spills coffee* *uses sock found in sleeve to mop it up*)

This is all to say, trust your instincts: This guy is probably a Schmagent.

But I bet your red hair really *is* fabulous.

Dear FYSA,

Everyone is so worried about getting an agent. I have another issue.

I've met agents at conferences who dress sloppy, look shabby, and speak in an unprofessional manner. How would they appear on my behalf walking into Macmillan? It's impossible to tell from a photo.

I've been published. I feel confident of my writing. I don't want an agent who says "like, uh" with every other word, and appears unpolished. Any suggestions on how to find an agent with presentation skills among his qualifications? What if you have a wonderful rapport via email and can't stand him when you meet face-to-face? Can a writer meet an agent in person before signing with him?

Best,
Concerned in California

Dear Concerned,

This is interesting, because it raises the question of what is the most important quality for an agent to have. I mean, I accessorize and am an accomplished public speaker, but I also once had a wheeled bar stool race with an award-winning author through the lobby of a Hyatt somewhere north of Chicago and south of sober. (But I *won*, and that is what is important in *that* story.)

But to begin to answer your question, one of my closest friends, Kelly Ceynowa, has her master's in organizational psychology, and at a recent conference she asked attendees who they'd be more comfortable having as their money manager, as they were shown pictures of a young Warren Buffett and a young Bernie Madoff. Mr. Buffett was dressed cheaply and looked perhaps a little unkempt, while Mr. Madoff was wearing an impeccable suit and tie. Overwhelmingly the audience picked Mr. Madoff—and we all know how *that* would have worked out for them. We already bring our own preconceptions to every interaction we have, so how can we ignore the instinct to team up with a representative who we feel best mirrors our own priorities?

I guess my question back to you would be, what *is* that priority: How an agent is *received* or how he is *perceived*? Meaning, if an agent seems unkempt and disorganized in person, but has a long and accomplished list of happy and well-placed clients, is that such a bad trade-off? Inversely, if an agent is well-groomed and silver-tongued, but after offering representation is reluctant to connect you to other clients for references, does that merit a larger red flag than no socks and a tendency to race bar stools?

If you queried this agent I assume there was something about her that made you feel she might make a strong advocate. But you don't have to sign with her if you don't feel she will ably represent you. The proof is in the puddin', whether the puddin' is a distinguished client list or, for a newer agent, a reputable agency, as it likely isn't adding cut-rate puddin' to its letterhead. As far as meeting in person before signing, I don't mind if I offer representation to someone and he flies out to meet with me first, but this would be expensive and, in my opinion, unnecessary. I bet you could learn a lot more about me and how I do my job by speaking to clients of mine who have been with me for years than you could from a thirty-minute face-to-face meeting in a bakery (which, obviously, is where we'd go to order the puddin').

Dear FYSA,

I've heard a lot of speculation in the writing groups I'm in about the "best" and "worst" times (of the week, of the day, even of the year) to query agents. Does timing really matter?

Curiously Yours,
Timekeeper

Dear Timekeeper,

Nah, there really isn't a "best" time. If pressed, I would say to *maaaaaaybe* avoid August and December? In the publishing industry, August is mint julep catch-up time and December is peppermint schnapps logjam time. Which is, incidentally, also the name of my bluegrass band.

But in the interest of information, I wanted to get a little deeper dive from others to give you a wholly informed response. Thus,

I committed to the obvious choice: I decided to slip incognito into the local watering hole to ask colleagues what their thoughts are regarding the best times to query. I chose to don a feather boa, galoshes, and a pith helmet so as to blend right in with the after-hours agent crowd.

It was clear within moments that no one suspected a thing. I sashayed up to the bar and casually asked New Leaf Literary & Media's Janet Reid (aka The Query Shark), "So, when *is* the best time to query you?"

Clearly comfortable speaking frankly in the presence of my boa, she spoke: "It's always tempting to think you can get a leg (or a fin) up by querying at just the right time. But everyone's schedule is different. Lots of agents work evenings, weekends, and holidays."

Folio Literary's Rachel Ekstrom chimed in: "I am as sporadic about responding to them as people are in sending them. I once startled someone by responding to their query at 4 A.M., but I was in an airport and had a chance to peek. Since agents read queries whenever they can (yes, we often don't have time during the workday), I think you can send them whenever you can." Then she offers this helpful caveat: "But never on a full moon, on account of the werewolfing. That always takes precedent."

But none of this is to say that timing doesn't wholly matter, as Root Literary's own Holly Root reminded us, en route to an unattended jar of maraschino cherries. "I'm a big believer that part of the magic of the query process *is* timing," she said. "In addition to your query enticing an agent, that agent has also got to be hungry for new projects, and that part is hard to time from the outside. If I've just sold the last of my unsold projects, I'm hitting the slush—whether it's August or December or April."

She makes an excellent point. There's industry-wide agreement with my thought that August and December aren't the best months because a lot of agents and editors use those notoriously slower publishing months to catch up on the submissions clogging their inboxes. Some agents (myself included) will occasionally even close to new queries during those times in order to completely clear the pipes. That said, I've also signed and sold things from my slush in those same months—such as G.S. Prendergast's brilliant young adult novel *Zero Repeat Forever*, which I signed on to represent on Dec. 7 and sold to Simon & Schuster at auction on Dec. 17. *Slow* doesn't mean *stopped*, and for the right book, *clearly* people don't have a problem getting their hustle on.

"The best time to query is when your project is ready to go," Reid said, adding, "The best agent to query is me first. Then Barbara Poelle." I almost blew my cover right there, but I covered quite admirably by muttering about a pith helmet emergency and excusing myself.

So query on, fair writers! I'll check my inbox as soon as I'm done with all this werewolfing.

Dear FYSA,

I and other aspiring writers have sent queries to agents and never heard a thing in response, not even a formulaic "not interested." This appears downright rude to me. Is this an accepted mode of "interaction" these days, and what are we to make of an agent who doesn't bother to respond to queries? I recognize that agents can get a lot of queries, but isn't that what keeps them in business?

Sincerely,
Empty Inbox

Dear Empty,

You nailed it: There's *gold* in them there query hills. About 60 percent of my list comes from unsolicited queries. And I truly sympathize with this complaint, as it is indeed something that bothers me as well. But, while there are of course agents out there who respond to each and every query, quite frankly, they are better humans than I for doing so.

Now, hear me out. I hired a fifth-grader to do my math for me, so I'm just ballparking here, but I get about seven to ten queries a day. Right now I have 967 of them in my email inbox. (Every one of those authors received an automatic reply from my account thanking them for choosing me, and saying that I will respond only if I am interested in seeing more.) Loosely speaking, out of every one hundred queries I receive, I will request three to four complete manuscripts. And only about one of every twenty-five to thirty manuscripts I request will result in me signing a new client.

Now, by those figures alone, you can see it takes a substantial amount of reading time on my part just to find a single author to add to my roster. That's in addition to the bulk of my job: working on behalf of my *current* clients. With a client list of about fifty to fifty-five now, even if I dedicate just an hour a week to each of those authors I've already committed to, I am at capacity for a "normal" workweek. Yes, yes, grab your tiny violin ... *Life for me is soooo haaaard* ... I mean, come on, I'm not saving lives or inventing toilet paper. (Wait, who invented toilet paper? Their face should be on the nickel or something.) But working with this equation, I have found that my time is better spent—and that I ultimately serve those who query me best—by fishing for the strongest material (in my subjective opinion) in the stack of queries I've received, and by requesting full manuscripts based on the queries I like best, and by burning the after-office hours reading those manuscripts, than it would be by tapping out a blanket form rejection 900 times.

But I hear what you're saying—and I feel the burning shame, I promise.

Dear FYSA,

Whoops! I realized that I accidentally attached my first chapter to a query when the submission guidelines specifically say to paste the first ten pages into the body of the email. What should I do? Is it okay to resubmit, following the correct procedure?

Signed,
This Bytes

Dear Bytes,

Let me begin by saying that I am not a computer expert—I only play one on TV—but in this age of viruses and malware masquerading as attached documents, I would bet that your pages weren't opened ... and, in fact, if the agent noticed that little paperclip icon in an unsolicited email, there's a good chance he deleted the query outright without even opening it. I advise you to re-send with the correct adherence to agency guidelines. You probably are telling yourself this by now, but I'll repeat it for the rest of the class: Attention to detail when querying is an important tool at your disposal to convey professionalism, so *always* double-check the guidelines before clicking *send*!

I kid you not, as I was typing this, my computer crashed and had to be restarted. I want to blame a virus attachment, but it might be all the Chris Hemsworth GIFs that I ... I mean, *someone* ... downloaded to my desktop.

Dear FYSA,

Do I have better odds querying a new agent than an established one? And if so, are there any downsides to targeting my queries exclusively to newer agents?

Yours,
Submission Stumped

Dear Stumped,

Take out a piece of paper and a pencil with one of those fuzzy-haired troll toppers on it (whatever happened to those?), and write "Confetti Cannon" on one side and "Laser Pens" on the other. Because essentially that's what we're talking about in comparing new agents to established ones.

When I was a baby agent staggering out in the meadow on spindly legs in the mid aughts, I had a lot of—what's the word for it?—oh right, *time*. I had the hours in my days and weeks to really dig into the slush, attend seven to ten conferences a year, read literary magazines, and find voices that, even if they didn't have the right plot, had the right *something*. When I connected with such a writer, I'd take the time to read his entire manuscript and then write lengthy letters discussing said manuscript and why its current incarnation might struggle on the shelves, discuss comparative titles, suggest further reading, and then maintain email contact to check in on works-in-progress.

When it came to the clients I did take on, I was lucky in that my agency had enough cache that even when *my* name was met with confusion by a prospective editor at a publishing house, the *agency's* name kept the phone line open. I was all dewy and fresh and my sleeves were perpetually rolled up. (When I think about it now, I just want to lie down.)

This is the "confetti cannon" aspect of a new agent: Basically, I would kick open a door, pull the trigger, and blast the room with glittery goodness, and then turn on the light to see what I hit. Then do it again in the next room. There is a lot to be said for the ferocious determination of a newbie.

Inversely, when I was a newbie, watching a more established agent like my boss work was like watching a hot butcher knife cut through butter. She has a laser-like approach in acquiring for and maintaining her client list. She knows what she wants when she finds it, and though she will *always* work tirelessly on something she loves, she has a specific elegance about the approach—an elegance that reflects her forty-plus years of cultivating relationships, developing a deep understanding of the market as well as the nuances of its many imprints, and negotiating the best possible deal terms for her clients.

One time, true story, I heard her say—dismissively and coolly—into the phone to an editor regarding an offer for a debut author, "That offer is simply un-American. Call me back with a more patriotic number." And she hung up. I almost swooned, because, I mean ... *What?!*

No really ... *WHAT??!*

But, when that editor called back she got her client to six figures. So while I would guess an established agent may take longer to respond to submissions, and may take longer to return clients' emails and calls (as they have a deeper client list), they might also get things read faster by editors, and ultimately be able to shake loose some deal points based on their stellar reputation.

Here's the thing, though: If you've got good stuff, your odds won't depend on who you send it to. I'd say the best thing to do is split your agent wish list between the two camps, and your work will pull the attention it warrants.

Dear FYSA,

A lot of agencies' websites say they read every query. But I could say the same thing about all the junk mail I receive. How much time do you really spend looking at each query—as in, average seconds per query letter? Give it to me straight. I can take it.

Signed,
Braced for It

Dear Braced,

This reminds me of the time I got curious and ordered my older sister Andee to hit me as hard as she could, to see if I could take it. She looks like Reese Witherspoon and weighs maybe 101 pounds soaking wet with rocks in her pockets, but she went ahead and cranked me a teeth-rattler on the arm that I feel fairly certain created some sort of embolism that is just waiting to travel to my brain like a gift that keeps on giving.

That is a preface to say: Ground yourself; this one might be a molar-shaker.

Sometimes it really is only, say, four seconds; a first line can close it down for me (e.g., the one I got that opened with, "What if it was your job to kill babies?"). Often the deal breaker is elsewhere in the first paragraph, when I see yet another Hezbollah/North Korea/China terrorist thriller plot. Or sometimes it's at a point later in a query when I am insulted, belittled, or offended (yup, those happen too).

In general, I just stop the second I realize the story is just not for me. But average time per query aside, I can assure you this: I *do* look at 'em.

Dear FYSA,

I have a list of dream agents to submit to, and there is one that I absolutely know is my perfect fit. I JUST KNOW IT! Can I say that in my query?

Sincerely,
Made4EachOther

Dear Made,

One time, I went on a first date with a guy we'll call RJ. We met at the restaurant, ordered drinks, and started chatting. While the appetizers were still on the table, RJ suddenly reached for my hand and said so sweetly, so sincerely: "Will it freak you out if I tell you I am already in love with you?"

Yup, RJ. Yup, it will. *It will totally freak me out.*

Thinking someone is your dream agent is based on observing how they have handled the careers of others. But all author career paths are filled with nuances and differences, so no matter what you perceive from outside observations, the conversations you will have with agents will help you determine who really *is* your love connection. That is not to say you won't end up with your dream weaver, but stay open to other interest, wait until you speak with all offering parties about how they envision your novel and the progression of your career before picking out china patterns.

Unless it's me, and I call you to offer. Then you can doodle combinations of my last name and yours as much as you want.

Dear FYSA,

How are queries received by agents for young adult fiction? Is there a taint? Or do they get the same consideration as other genres?

Sincerely,
Untainted Love

Dear Untainted,

Are you referring to rumored misconceptions that young adult is somehow easier to write, or that YA authors are in any way less capable than adult authors? Quite the contrary! YA is a robust and varied market, and if anything the readers are more voracious and loyal than in other areas of the bookstore. Think about a readership hopped up on hormones and angst, still willing to believe in magic and very able to call out heroes *and* posers on vast social media forums. *That's* a stadium for some truly spectacular storytellers to show their best moves.

YA authors, like those in any other genre, need to put blood, sweat, and tears into every word. (If you're #1 *New York Times* bestseller Kerri Maniscalco, lots and lots of blood.) But this would be obvious to everyone writing in the genre as they are also aggressively *reading* in the genre ... right? And not just focusing on the bestsellers, but taking the time to read titles of lesser fame, to ask librarians (those brilliant Book Buddhas, those gorgeous Genre Gurus) for recommendations.

So rest assured that submissions from *all* desired genres get the same consideration in the inbox—the writing is the only thing that can "taint" a submission. Even if a query is a little wobbly on the dismount but has a grain of something that rings a bell with me, I will dip into the writing to see what's there, and that's where all decisions begin and end.

Dear FYSA,

I know writers who have had mixed results connecting with literary agents at conferences and on social media. What are the most viable ways to make meaningful, personal contacts with agents outside of the slush pile?

Sincerely,
Craving Connections

Dear Craving Connections,

Upward of 60 percent of my clients came from slush, so I still feel that is the most viable method of contact. Conferences and social media *can* work, if done correctly—but there are recommended ways to get your work in front of an agent, and then there are ways that are, well, not so recommended. Your ultimate goal is always the same—to write the work that stands out from the rest of the penguin suits with its sequined top hat and fuchsia tails—but the delivery system can vary, and you want to make sure you put your best face forward, not the one that has runny mascara and those creepy bits of dried saliva at the corners of its mouth from scream crying into a pillow.

And so without further ado, I now present to you: Poelle's Agent Contact Methods List: Fancy Penguins vs. Scream Crying Into a Pillow, with each method ranked with the appropriate number of fancy penguins or, inversely, of tissues crumpled from scream crying.

- **CRITIQUE PARTNERS: 5 FANCY PENGUINS.** If you are a writer, you scribble away and make wonderful stories. If you are going to become an *author*, you also belong to a writing community where you organically cultivate resources and form partnerships. Tap into your loop, using beta readers and critique partners you can trust to make your work better. Then, if possible, take it a step further: Do you have agented authors among those supporters? Can you get an honest referral from each of them? Can you ask them to go even further and *call* their agent and say, "Can you take a look at my friend Bob's work?" When my people call, I listen.
- **COMING UNSOLICITED TO THE AGENT'S OFFICE: 5 SCREAM-CRY TISSUES.** Don't do this. Especially don't do this dressed as your protagonist. From the future.
- **THROUGH THE ACKNOWLEDGMENTS PAGE: 4 FANCY PENGUINS.** While you are reading 2,000 published words in your genre for every 2,000 words you write (as it goes without *question* that you are doing, right?) take a moment to flip to the

Acknowledgments page and see who the agent is. This is a good list to keep to help make a query stand out or an intro at a conference be grounded in something other than that weird blind date feeling. "After reading *The Guilty One* by Sophie Littlefield, I felt this might be in your wheelhouse as my manuscript is also upmarket suspense ..." It gives an educated edge to your approach.

- **BECOMING YOUR OWN AGENT: 4 SCREAM-CRY TISSUES.** I have heard urban legends of such things (where an author calls an editor under a fake name and represents his own work) but never a firsthand story. I would think this would be hard to do for a multitude of reasons, though. Like, what happens if the editor wants to speak to the author? How do you do conference calls? But most important, the main obstacle to pitching your own work directly to publishers would be that it is challenging to match the timbre of the agent pitch: It is a precise combination of vodka-before-noon meets stevedore-speak with an underlying dash of ennui. And that ain't easy. (Seriously, trust me when I say that imitators will be revealed as such, and when it happens, you will not be applauded for your creativity.)
- **SOCIAL MEDIA PRESENCE: 2 FANCY PENGUINS.** I'm not talking about friending agents on Facebook. I'm talking about, as part of your interactions with people you like and know, talking about how the progress on your novel is coming, so that when you finish, you have a network of folks who are genuinely rooting for you—and who may have contacts themselves. I've had many non-publishing friends reach out to me and say they have a friend who is shopping a manuscript and ask me to take a peek. And I love to have my friends owe me ... er, I mean, I love to help out a friend, and if that means I take a peek at three chapters, so be it. Also? It doesn't hurt to enlist

your social network to hold you accountable for finishing the book in the first place.

- **MY AGENCY QUERY INBOX: 5 FANCY PENGUINS.** You wanna put your manuscript where my mouth is? Wait, that came out creepy. But here's what I suggest: If you have a *very polished*, finished manuscript in a genre we represent, send the right person in my agency your query letter and the first ten pages in the body of an email with the subject line FIVE FANCY PENGUINS, and let's see what happens. Our query inboxes are [firstname.queries@irenegoodman.com]. Life is about taking chances—don't come scream crying to me if you pass this one up!

Dear FYSA,

What do you really think of speed-pitching events at conferences? Do you secretly hate them? And how many of your new authors do you find at writing conferences, versus the slush pile, versus other methods?

Signed,
Running the Numbers

Dear Numbers,

Well, let's see. Here are some things that have happened to me at speed-dating-style pitch sessions:

- After I said I would not be interested in looking at a man's poetry collection, he said he would kill himself—and the police had to be called.
- An octogenarian and his wife pitched his mystery and she mouthed his memorized pitch next to him the whole time he talked, and then clapped *and cried* when he was done—and

I had to sit there knowing from the start that a 42,000-word World War II mystery (which is far too short to be viable, for starters) was something I was for sure about to say no to. To this octogenarian's life dream. In front of his lifelong *soul mate.*

- A woman sat down across from me and opened with, "Jesus already told me you would be my agent, so I'm not nervous at all." I said, "That's weird, when we had coffee the other day, he didn't mention you." And then I chuckled. She did *not.* And then my bladder loosened a bit in fear.

In the end, I very much like talking to authors at conferences, but I wouldn't buy a car from a guy who just tells me about it; I need to see how she rides. So these days, when I'm invited to participate in pitch sessions at writing events I decline. Instead I will do panels and workshops where I repeatedly announce my query email. That way everyone feels like they got a request and will get their work in front of someone for thoughtful consideration. Of course authors can also gain valuable requests at pitch sessions, but you won't find me in those rooms. In my opinion they are just too much pressure on the authors. And my bladder.

Dear FYSA,

When I follow an agent into the bathroom at a conference, should I pitch before, after, or while I wash my hands?

Sincerely,
Kidding (Or Am I?)

Dear Kidding (Or Are You?),

I would prefer to not be approached at the urinal. Anything else is fair game.

Dear FYSA,

Do you receive exclusive queries, and if so, do you give them preference? How long is an appropriate time period for a writer to grant an agent an exclusive? Is six weeks within reason?

Sincerely,
Exclusively Yours

Dear Exclusively Mine,

I do from time to time receive unsolicited exclusive queries, and this always confuses me. Appearing in someone's inbox and granting them an exclusive read as a first time author just doesn't make sense. For starters, many agents are a good six to eight weeks [*cough cough or a lot longer cough*] behind in reviewing submissions, so by the time they get to your offer of exclusivity it has expired. Also, agents generally expect that the queries they receive are being submitted elsewhere simultaneously. So why needlessly limit your book's prospects to a single stranger sitting across the table, when you could instead send her out e-speed dating and then collect the list of gentleman callers who are truly interested in order to find the best suitor?

Now this is a lipstick of a different color: If I meet someone or get a referral and I read the first few chapters and *then ask* for an exclusive read of the full manuscript, I did so because I feel good about what I have already read. And when I do that I ask for, at the most, seventy-two hours, perhaps planning to read it over a weekend. I don't want to keep the author in a state of suspended animation only to dash both our hopes by passing on something a month and a half later when they could have been submitting it elsewhere.

My advice: Never *offer* an exclusive, and if one is requested, keep the time frame to a minimum.

Dear FYSA,

A writer friend recommended that I cross all agents who are not based in New York off of my wish list. Are there really disadvantages to being represented by an agent who lives elsewhere?

Sincerely,
Geographically Challenged

Dear Geo,

My agency is located in New York City, but just for funsies, here is a list of a few of the many locations I've negotiated deals from: Cabo San Lucas, Mexico; intermission at a Broadway Show; a neonatal intensive care unit; in a rented van named Jerry outside of Salem, Mass.; and a Starbucks somewhere off the Grapevine pass between Los Angeles and San Francisco.

Sara Megibow is an agent with KT Literary Agency in Colorado and routinely compels me to send her envious emails lamenting the brilliant deals she executes. Holly Root and Root Literary are on the West Coast, and her deals adorn *The Hollywood Reporter* and *Publishers Weekly* alike. So no, an agent's ZIP code shouldn't matter as long as she is a professional who knows who to connect with in the genres she represents.

When you are considering an offer, ask the kinds of questions you want your literary agent to be able to answer, not the kind that Google Earth can.

The one thing I will say, though, is that no matter where their offices are, I *personally* feel that agents should come to New York City at least once a year, if able, in order to have face-to-face meetings with editors and publishers; even better if those visits coincide with events like the Writer's Digest Conference, Society of Children's Book Writers & Illustrators Conference, the Edgar awards, or ThrillerFest, so they also have an opportunity to converse with clients and other agents in order to keep a presence on the scene.

They could even rent Jerry and make a road trip out of it.

Dear FYSA,

When I started querying agents for my novel, I got several requests for full and partial manuscripts. The feedback I received was positive, though the novel was eventually rejected by all but three of them, who did not reply. After several months, I followed up with an email to those three (who had two fulls and one partial). One responded within a couple weeks with another rejection, but lots of praise. I've not heard from the other two.

My question is: How much prodding and/or follow-up should I do? Should I re-query these same agents, or just move on to the next group? My fear is that the manuscript went to an intern who is no longer at the company. Not only would the manuscript be buried in a slush pile, but the slush pile of a nonexistent person.

What do you advise?

Sincerely,
Hanging in Limbo

Dear Limbo,

Congratulations: The fact that you're getting requests for partials and fulls means, at the very least, that you have something in the foundation of your work (such as good timing or an intriguing plot) that appeals to your target agents, so that is half the battle. Following up by sending a nudge six to eight weeks later? Right again! You have absolutely done your part to get the manuscript in front of agents who could be a fit. So, if someone misses the banquet of brilliance you have served them, that is their fork to stab themselves in the face with. (You'll notice my own tine scars *here* and *here*.)

In this case, send one more nudge to the silent folks, just to satisfy that itch, but then get your query out to another fifteen agents—and *then*, drop and give me another 1,000 words on your work-in-progress. Just as today's interns are tomorrow's agents, today's WIP could be tomorrow's meal ticket (fork not included).

Dear FYSA,

I recently received critiques of the first chapter of my middle-grade novel from two veteran literary agents. That was great. The problem is that in several places the agents gave me advice that contradicted the advice of the other. For example: Agent 1 said a piece of description was wonderful and really helped the reader get into the story. Agent 2 said the same description was too detailed, added "fluff," and wasn't needed. How does one decide on a path of revision given contradictory recommendations?

Best,
Lost in Contradiction

Dear Lost,

Ain't that the rub? This is why I add some form of "subjectively speaking" to all of my own responses. Each agent has a different angle on what is going to make it to the competitive shelves. If you're at the beginning of your submissions process and these two agents aren't offering the feedback in the context of an offer for representation, then I would suggest that more data is needed before you revise. Look for a common thread among feedback from a wide sampling of agents before driving yourself crazy taking every single piece of criticism to heart.

If, however, for some reason you were going to use the responses from only these two agents to shape your revision, or if these two agents are both offering to represent the work provided you follow their suggested path for revision, pull on the thread that resonates with you the most. (Have you been told before that you tend to "overwrite"? Or have you been told before that your descriptions are atmospheric?) Follow your instincts on what you feel could benefit your craft.

Dear FYSA,

While I understand that novels need to be complete before submission, why then can nonfiction be pitched as unfinished work, with only a proposal, outline, and sample chapters? And if an agent or publisher likes the idea, what is considered a reasonable turnaround time for the completed manuscript?

Sincerely,
Nonfiction Nonplussed

Dear Nonplussed,

Aside from memoir and other narrative forms—which occasionally follow the same submission protocol as novels, because of their reliance on craft elements such as voice, style, and story arcs to be successful—nonfiction can be pitched with a proposal because it is significantly reliant on platform and premise. When you are tackling a topic rather than a theme, an outline coupled with sample chapters is enough to give agents and publishers a solid idea of what the finished product would be. We care about the overall appeal of the subject matter, the qualifying factors of the author that enable her to speak with authority on said subject matter, and the market need for a book (or yet another book) on this subject matter. If I can make a case for all three of those factors, I can easily work with an author on shaping up the voice and pacing to prepare for pitching with just a proposal.

From the time the book is acquired, then, turnaround time is generally six to nine months, unless the subject matter dictates a timeline, either by being zeitgeist-y and therefore more immediate for the marketplace, or related to a certain event, such as an election or the Olympics (in which case you may have even more time).

Meanwhile, yes, (exempting of course, option material for continuing a contract) I wish I could just call editors about a client's fiction and say, "It's about a fire marshal, certain that his pyromaniac wife is the one setting lethal fires in New Orleans, and the lines he is willing to cross to protect her until he realizes ... something that the author will tell us when she gets to it." Because even if that author had a proven track record writing fiction, I have been told by many of my novelist clients that they "didn't know" a plot point until they got to it, and so I'm not as confident pitching a novel from an author before it's complete. It's not unusual for plot twists and even hidden antagonists to reveal themselves only as the book is being written.

Also? Uh, I really want to read that fire marshal book. Someone get on that (*looks pointedly at Sharon Doering*).

Dear FYSA,

Are agents really more interested in authors working on series than authors of stand-alone books? I've been told that's why mine has never been picked up.

Signed,
Only the Standalonely

Dear Standalonely,

I was once told that all U.S. presidents have to be assassinated when they leave office. And then I presented that fact in my second-grade report on Abraham Lincoln. At which point my teacher actually stopped the presentation and yelled at me. I then went home and told my sister Andee what happened. At which point she rolled her fifth-grade eyes and said, "*Doofus*, I was joking." And then she punched me in the arm.

So you see, don't believe everything you hear.

I have sold stand-alone books and series across the board, and whether or not there is a franchise possibility has nothing to do with my consideration of representation whatsoever. Just be good. I like that part the best.

Dear FYSA,

How willing are agents to represent a novel that falls into more than one genre? I'm not talking about subgenres like "romantic suspense," but something that can't be pegged easily. I'm curious as to what the stats are these days, because I see an awful lot of published books that fall in between the cracks of two, three, or even four genres. It seems the marketing could get complicated for this kind of book. Do agents have a tendency to shy away from books that pose a marketing challenge, or are they beginning to embrace them more often?

Signed
Genre Bender

Dear Bender,

Wait, this question confuses me a bit. What books are falling *between* four different genres? But I know a lot of writers have questions about genre-straddling books, so here is what I *will* say: If you are unable to tell me what it is you're writing (and do not say you "really can't" because "it has never been done before," because every time an author says that, a kitten explodes) then how am I going to frame it and sell it? There are of course subgenres within genres, but an author straddling too many genres is akin to a Sharktobear lurching out of the ocean, growling and biting and thrashing its eight arms hither and thither. And no one wants to approach that—not an agent, not a publisher, and not Greenpeace.

Dear FYSA,

I'm confident in my novel and query, have had several requests for the full ms, and even one conversation with an agent, but I can't seem to land representation. What are the top obstacles that writers face when trying to secure an agent, and how would you suggest they overcome them?

Signed,
Newbie in New York

Dear Newbie,

Recently, my husband and I started golf lessons together. His swing seemed to improve at an exponential rate, while my cursing did the same, in almost a direct ratio. I finally hollered at our absolutely unflappable British golf instructor, "What am I doing wrong?" He said dryly, "A little bit of everything. But that means you're also doing a little bit of everything *right*."

So, let's assume we can apply that to you. Let's even say that you're doing a lot of everything right. Treating this as a par three, I'm going to take three swings at what might be the issue at hand:

1. THE DRIVER. Let's say that you indeed have a strong query and a well-written novel that falls within the appropriate word count for your genre—a solid drive right down the fairway. But the gal two rounds earlier? She crushed it. And the guy after her? He also crushed it. Like, almost to the green. So while this may be your very best effort and a book you're proud of, the agent has already seen some work in her inbox that set the bar *really* high that day, and therefore didn't request your full. Remember, you should be querying twenty-five to thirty agents. Only after getting a data set from that many subjective responders can you determine it's time to set this aside and switch focus to your current WIP.

2. THE FIVE IRON. Now let's say you crushed it. Almost to the green. You have a solid query and a very well-written novel. But maybe it's a family-oriented drama with suspenseful elements, or middle-grade fantasy. The market is very crowded with these subgenres right now. That's not to say there isn't room for more. Even though your book is absolutely on track with what's out there now, agents and editors may already have several on their list for the next few publication seasons. Again, the solution here is to keep reading in your genre, pay attention to what else is out there and what (if any) revisions you might apply to stand out. *And*, keep querying—when "trends" are afoot, it means that while a lot of people *have* such books on their list, a lot of other people *want* them on their list.

3. THE PUTTER. This time you have a solid query, a well-written novel, a request for a full, *and* an email from an agent who wants to chat on the phone. You're on the green. Here are my guesses as to why you're not sinking the putt. Maybe you're missing a synopsis/log line for your *next* novel. Agents don't want to just sell a book, they want to represent a *career*. By the time you're at the submission phase, you should be prepared to talk about your follow-up idea in a succinct manner.

Or maybe you were resistant to editorial thoughts presented by the agent. That doesn't mean you're in the wrong, but if an agent isn't feeling 100 percent enthusiastic about the work *without* those edits, then they aren't the agent for you anyway. Once I had what seemed like a wonderful editorial call with an author. The next day she sent an email saying my edits "scared her," because she didn't think she could follow through on them. Right there, I agreed with her that it wasn't the best fit. I don't want to present work to editors that I think still needs revision. And if *my* edits scared her, an editor would send her screaming into the night.

Now, join me at my favorite part of the golf course: the 19th hole. If we were throwing back G&Ts and lying about our golf scores, I would also remind you it ain't easy, this writing game. Your first novel may not drop in the hole. Nor your second. Nor fifth. The biggest obstacle one can have in publishing is quitting. If you're going to do a little bit right, have that little bit be the fact that you don't quit.

Dear FYSA,

For the past few months I've been reviewing publishing deals in industry reports. Can you explain the term "exclusive submission"?

Best,
Parsing Words

Dear Parsing,

Much obliged! When preparing your manuscript for submission to editors at imprints of publishing houses, a plan will start to form in my mind based on a variety of factors. I'll talk over my strategy with you, discussing it in detail and being very open to input … meaning I will call you and bark, "This is what I'm doing, Stan!" regardless of whether or not your name is Stan. But you'll be okay, Stan, because you will now be informed about *why* I think this particular plan is the best one to get you headed down that publishing path.

One such strategy might be to give someone an "exclusive" look. This could mean they're the only editor at a publishing house being sent the manuscript for consideration, or it can mean they are the only editor in *all of publishing* that has it. Usually these exclusive periods will come with a deadline (sometimes forty-eight hours, sometimes a week).

This "exclusive look" is the strategy I formed for Samantha Downing's debut novel, *My Lovely Wife*. I had recently met newly Acquiring Editor Jen Monroe at Berkley (an imprint under the Penguin Random House umbrella), and we just clicked. When Downing's deliciously haunting manuscript came to me a few weeks later, I was struck that not only did it seem like exactly the type of book Jen and I had discussed we were both looking for—but that Jen, as a newly acquiring editor, had the enthusiasm and the *bandwidth* to take a chance on an exclusive look with a tight deadline. I talked it over with Sam and explained that if Jen went for it, great! But also if Jen *didn't* go for the book, we'd agreed that she would provide comprehensive reasoning behind the pass, which would give Sam and I feedback to consider before we went wider.

Jen was overjoyed to have the exclusive look. I gave her forty-eight hours—all alone, in all of publishing—and that woman put the "us" in hustle. She got team support (so essential in any acquisition these days), and came back with a six-figure offer. The author and I considered that offer to be "pre-emptive," meaning we felt it was exactly what we wanted and was enough of a show of support that we could accept without feeling the need to shop the manuscript around any further. And thus we plucked the fruits of the exclusive labors.

See? It's good to have a plan, Stan.

Dear FYSA,

If a writer, on his own, is unsuccessful in directly querying publishers who accept unsolicited submissions, can he later resubmit his work to those same publishers through an agent?

Best,
Double Dipping in Detroit

Dear Double Dipper,

Well, when an author signs with an agent, *the author* won't be submitting the work anywhere—the agent will be handling all submissions. I think that's what you meant, but just in case it's not, I want to share an unfortunate experience I had several years ago. After I had explained to a newly signed client in detail why I wouldn't be resubmitting her work to an imprint that had previously passed on her unsolicited manuscript, the author took it upon herself to *call the editor*, say I was now her agent, and then *re-pitch her novel* to the editor—who was terribly confused and flustered and then, of course, hung up and called me immediately to let me know this had happened. We concluded the call by mutually acknowledging this was not the type of material they were looking to acquire, regardless of the author's breach of etiquette. And the fun was just beginning! While on *that* call, I got a voicemail from another editor saying that my client had just called *her* and pitched the same material ... which was also not appropriate for *her* imprint! Wheee! My next action was to call and sever representation with the author. Well, actually the very next thing I did was use some "lazy words." *Then* I called and severed representation. If I can't be trusted to do my job correctly at this early stage of knowing where to send your book and why, it isn't worth the agony for either of us.

The black-and-white answer to your question is no: If you've submitted on your own and received a pass, that does not necessarily mean you've shut the door on the imprint/publisher as a whole. It may have been the wrong editor at the wrong time.

What is appropriate here is to tell the agent where the manuscript has been and to what extent it was received, and to, of course, inform the agent of any other contacts made through conference requests or writer referrals. The agent should then discuss with you in detail why pursuing these outlets would be supportive to your overall career plan, or not.

If the agent feels that there is a reason to return to an imprint, then she will doggedly pursue it. In my case, I might call and say, "Hey, LaShell, full disclosure: Jerry saw this several months ago unsolicited, but it's been through a major revision, and I know when I saw you last week you mentioned you were on the hunt for horror with a speculative twist ..." *This* is why you get an agent: to have an advocate for your work who knows how to get better responses and results than you could on your own, whether that's at a market you've already thought of or a new one entirely.

Dear FYSA,

I queried my novel to a handful of agents (none were interested) before realizing it wasn't ready yet and needed some major revisions. Would it be inappropriate to re-query any of them when my new-and-improved novel is ready to submit? It's going through significant changes (I'm editing out a main character), so will be fundamentally different from the novel they turned down.

Sincerely,
Query-ous

Dear Query-ous,

I wanted to write a concise and knowledgeable response to this question, but that was hard to do after my head exploded. Can any of you out there in the studio audience guess why my office has gone from matte white to matter gray?

Did anyone come up with the line ... "*before realizing it wasn't ready yet and needed some major revisions*"? Oh, great. I retyped it and now my pancreas exploded.

I'm not harping on the fact that the manuscript wasn't 100 percent "ready yet." Even when I'm shopping a client's manuscript, there may be a whiff of a nuance of unreadiness—one that can be remedied as a matter of process when the project finds a home with a skillful editor. The idea that *major revisions* were *needed* to make it *fundamentally different* is why I'm currently wearing a helmet to hold in the remainder of my thoughts.

Look, I am *not* known for being ... hesitant. If I ever write a novel, I'll probably type "El Fin!" and then send it off—and *then* realize I forgot to fix every misuse of *affect/effect*. And also that I forgot to wear pants in running out for a celebratory beverage. Waiting is not my thing. So if you relate, I get it. But when I read your question, I fear your situation could speak to a larger issue: an absence of the investment in a community of similarly skilled writers who can serve as partners, who can catch the major problems that need to be addressed *before* you shoot your work from the trebuchet of your outbox into the laps of your first-round choices for representation. And the chorus sings: CRITIQUE PARTNER!

Writing may be a solitary endeavor, but a writer's intent is to tell a story—and storytellers by their very nature need someone on the receiving end. Your first choices of agents should not be your guinea pigs. Do you now, if you didn't before, have trusted readers in place for your newly revised manuscript? If not, history may be doomed to repeat itself. Attending conferences, creating a circle of fellow writers, reading in your genre and trading feedback on the works of others who are standing on your same career step will greatly improve your odds of having the opportunity to identify and revise significant issues before submission.

Live and learn. I can speak only for myself, but if I do not specifically request that you revise and resubmit, I would not be interested in seeing a return to my inbox. Take heart, however, that a handful of agents is barely scratching the surface. There are many wonderful reps out there, and I hope that you do submit to a new batch ... *after* you have feedback from trusted partners.

Dear FYSA,

When I look around writing conferences, I see lots of gray hair. Are there really agents and editors who will take a chance on older writers like me with a first novel? And will you automatically reject a book based on education or lack thereof? Do you ever judge a book regarding the writer's age?

Yours,
In the Golden Years

Dear Golden,

What? Okay, wait, *WHAT? NO.* If I could write the word *no* larger and maybe set the letters on fire, I would. The only thing I ever judge writers by is *obviously* their looks. I mean, have you *seen* my clients? Go look up Graham Brown's website right now. I'll wait.

Told you.

But I hear you ... and isn't it odd and sad to think there would be any real reason for your concern? But there is undoubtedly some unnamed, unsourced pressure to publish young. I'll tell you, though, it ain't coming from me. Like the vast majority of my agenting colleagues, I recognize that there is no age that can be applied to the ripening of a story that is ready to be told. It doesn't matter if you're 18 or 85; if the story is intriguing and the writing is captivating, it's time to take a chance on the author. Just write a fabulous book, and no one will count the candles on your next cake.

Dear FYSA,

Lots of agent guidelines say that if one representative at a larger agency says no to your query, then it's a no from everyone else there, too. But I'm really skeptical that agents actually share queries/ manuscripts with their colleagues. Is this just their way of being dismissive?

Sincerely,
Don't BS With Me

Dear BS Detector,

Ah, there it is. The nuanced question that requires finesse, deftness, and grace to execute. Let me just dust off the Dorito shrapnel and swallow this belch into my fist before proceeding.

If I get a submission that isn't in my wheelhouse (new adult, *really* commercial women's fiction, graphic novel, Amish romance, etc.) but that I think has promise, I absolutely forward it to a colleague who is better suited to said work. I have even gone so far as to work on a manuscript with an author, still not feel like it hits the right notes with my subjective taste, and *then* pass it along to a colleague—sometimes with resounding success! And my colleagues have done the same for me.

Agents who work together, or who know each other's work, build that trust with one another through experience, and as an author, you can trust in that process as well. None of us in the business of author representation want to *prevent* a career. With every query I open, I hope it's *the one*, and I remain optimistic until something shows me it isn't. I can often recognize that "something" on behalf of other colleagues too. There simply isn't a downside to passing along a query or manuscript that *does* have potential to my able coworkers.

Dear FYSA,

When querying a previous manuscript, I received requests for fulls and then personalized rejections from agents I'd now like to query for a new manuscript. What is the etiquette for querying those agents? Can I use first names? If the agent receives queries at one email address and corresponds with writers at another, can I use the direct email for the new query? Should I mention the positive comments the agent made about the writing in my previous manuscript?

Sincerely,
Second Time Around

Dear Second Timer,

Personally, I'm good with "Barbara" no matter the round of submission, as we ostensibly could be co-workers. But no nicknames, please. Other agents might prefer to keep things more formal; take your cue from the previous correspondence.

At the bottom of your email, include the most recent exchange with the agent, so the reminder of your previous correspondence will appear below your query (I love it when an author includes our previous back-and-forth to support why he is reconnecting—it is an immeasurable help). Do use the email address indicated for queries *unless* the agent invited you to submit again. Perhaps open with a line stating that you are querying this agent with a new project because you found his feedback on your last full manuscript to be both generous and helpful, and then jump right in.

Dear FYSA,

I pitched my novel to a St. Martin's Press editor at a conference. "I'm intrigued," he said. "Submit it to me through an agent." Should I mention in my queries that it's been requested by this editor? I've queried half a dozen agents and it doesn't seem to matter whether I've included that info. All I collect are encouraging rejections.

Sincerely,
Stuck at the Gate

Dear Stuck at the Gate,

Telling a prospective agent you have an editor's request shows: 1.) You have interest from a viable entity, and 2.) You attend conferences and thus are invested in furthering your career rather than relying on just hope as a marketing tool.

That said ... Wait. Step over here and sip from my flask until your loins feel all girded up. Ready? Okay. That said, having a request from an editor isn't going to make or break a query. The agent's response still comes down to that dang darn ol' writing.

And further (help yourself to another medicinal swig!), should that editor have received a sample from you on the spot (i.e., not just a verbal pitch), *if* he'd felt the idea was superb and the writing was engaging, he *might* have asked to take a peek at the rest anyway and then referred you to a handful of trusted reps. *But not always.* Sometimes. *But not every time.* I've seen it. *But not every day.*

In a nutshell: Yes. Mention *any* requests garnered in the query. Mention any author blurbs or marketing reaches you already have, too. Put in everything your manuscript needs you to say for it because it cannot speak for itself ... until it does. With the writing.

Dear FYSA,

I'm on the verge of sending queries for a humor novel. Although the book is supposed to be funny, what about the query? I'm thinking of the paragraph that is meant to sum up its premise and demonstrate that I know how to tell a story. Should it contain humor in the style of the book? Or would the agent consider this to be a distraction—or even unprofessional?

Sincerely,
Funny Business

Dear Funny Business,

From the soprano section of the choir, I yell, "Amen, Preacher!" No matter the situation, I am unable to *not* funny it up. ("Yes, Barbara, hilarious. Now please sit down, as the family would like to view the body.")

I must be *exhausting.*

Here's the thing: If you and I were to break down what "funny" is, we might have different descriptions of what gets the yuks, but in the end, it all comes down to timing. In person, there is a certain agility humorists have that almost seems to bend time to allow for them to think of something funny in a split second. When there is an added luxury of the ability to put it on paper, revise, and ponder, the humorous writer can really shine ... maybe too brightly for her own good. Being funny, pithy, irreverent, or raunchy in a query may actually undermine what you are trying to do—which is essentially to prove that you not only have something to say but an appealing and educated way to say it.

There is a rhythm to humor, as in music, where beats and moments fuel and support a witticism or punch line, and comedians and humor writers walk around with that instrument *always* pressed to their lips. It's how they stand out and how they hide. It's how they connect and how they keep their distance. It's how they comfort and how they injure. In essence, true humorists cannot help it—the funny will happen. We are desperate folks who need that affirmation. It's a seven-course meal for the ego and more addictive than heroin.

I would suggest, therefore, that when it comes to the query for anything humorous, fiction or otherwise, the best course of action is to have the intent of a straightforward query. Because there will undoubtedly be a moment or two of levity that sneaks in. You are a balloon full of funny, and the world is a cactus—it's going to leak.

So try to keep the query as professional as possible to get the agent or editor to the actual pages. Then unleash the banana cream pie.

Dear FYSA,

I've been with my agent a few years and we've made some modest (and one not so modest!) sales, but lately I feel like the relationship has become stagnant. I don't have a specific complaint, but just feel like I'm being shuffled to the end of the line, priority-wise. How can you tell when it's time to move on to new representation?

Sincerely,
She's Just Not That Into Me

Dear She's Not Into You,

The closest comparable relationship to that of the author/agent is a marriage. I know that sounds cliché, but so does "mommy needs wine" and I just bellowed that across the room, so there *is* truth in well-trodden words. It is all about feeling mutually respected in the role you play within the system, and when that starts to feel unstable, that is where these little red flags start to appear.

I have dropped clients and I have been dropped by clients. (What? *I know.* Don't they know who I think I am?) And I'd venture a guess that neither side is ever *truly* surprised to get that call. There are bumps that pop up, communications missed that confetti the publishing path enough that it's hard to ignore the shuffling of paper shreds at your feet. No one falls out of bed in the morning and thinks, *Imma do some self-sabotage today and start dumping folks!* with a whistle and a grin. Thus I'd suggest there are subtle signals on *both* sides that such a conversation is on the horizon.

So, without further ado, I present: How to Initiate This Conversation With Your Agent.

We begin with a voicemail left by Nancy No-No, who is feeling especially ignored by her agent:

Nancy: "Hello, Agent? It's your client, Nancy [hic] No-No. When you signed me [hic] I was shiny and new and now ... now ... [sounds of sobbing] *now you hate me and I know it.*"

And here comes Patty Perfect, who has also been disappointed with her agent's lack of communication. Let's listen in on her call:

Patty: "Hi, Agent. As I said in my email, I just wanted a quick check-in chat today, so thanks for setting aside the time. I haven't been feeling as confident in our arrangement and I wanted to touch base about that."

I think we can agree that Patty pulled this one off a little better. And that we all knew Nancy in college.

As the call progresses, here are the reasons why Nancy thinks she might need to fire her agent:

"Becky Betterthan got a higher advance for her book than I did, and her novel reads like someone barfed up alphabet soup."

"You didn't get [Canadian cover approval/85 percent e-book rights split] in my contract."

"For every one tweet to me you tweet other authors 2.35 percent more."

In contrast, let's take a look at the reasons that Patty is outlining in *her* call:

"I'm waiting too long to hear from you when I have questions—I don't think I should have to anticipate a week or more for a reply. Even a simple 'I'll get back to you' would be appreciated."

"I'm not being kept up-to-date on where my manuscript is being submitted or the responses you've received. I'm not even sure if you've gone out with it yet."

> "My WIP has been in your 'To Read' pile for two months. I want to be someone that my agent is excited to read."
>
> "I don't feel like there is a strategy in place for short- and long-term career goals."

Wow! Patty really has her shit together.

You might find that this conversation leads to improved communication and is just what was needed to salvage the relationship. But if after this convo you're still not feeling positive about the partnership, then it's probably time to consult your original agency agreement and review the steps necessary to sever representation. Take note of the specific termination terms outlined, such as how much time the agent is allotted to wrap up any outstanding rights on offers, then send a kind, simple email to cut things off. (Some agency contracts do require that you follow that with a certified letter, so check the fine print.)

Once that's done, start tapping on doors and getting author referrals to find someone new to partner with.

Wait, what's that? You have to sever ties *before* you find a new agent? Wouldn't it be better to see if someone else is interested before you cut ties? Isn't it a little scary to have to play the field again?

It might be scary, but it's in everyone's best interest. No one comes out looking good when swinging like a drunken monkey in short pants from one agent to the next.

I can tell you, I won't even *speak* to an author if he is still represented elsewhere. I've turned away some big clients because I wasn't willing to have even an initial conversation while they were still technically under agreement. It's important for me to know that a new client has treated his former agent with professional courtesy and respect. Which isn't hard to do. Even in short pants.

Dear FYSA,

I've queried several agents representing my genre, and the rejections have been kind, but seem to say the same thing: It isn't for them, the industry is very subjective, or it just doesn't fit their personal taste. Are they just being nice, or is it literally just that?

Sincerely,
It's Not Personal

Dear Not Personal,

Husband has spent a lot of time hauling me through museums the way one hauls a stubborn Saint Bernard to the vet. On one particular excursion to a modern art show, I spent the initial twenty minutes wandering through muttering, "I don't get it," and, "This is just a pile of mannequin legs." Then, I stumbled upon an installation that consisted of what appeared to be a door in the wall. Piped in from behind it was the sound of dishes clanking, the sizzle and spit of a stovetop, men's voices above tinny music—and, as if I'd fallen through a wormhole, I was immediately in the back kitchen of every restaurant I've ever worked in. The cackle of a knife against the chopping board, the frustratingly slippery non-slip floor pads, the whoosh of steam from the dishwasher.

I beckoned madly to Husband and, literally bouncing with joy, said, "This one is awesome! It's like a time machine to my twenties! I totally get it! I totally get modern art!"

After a beat where I presume a *lot* happened for him internally, Husband said, "That's actually a door to the kitchen."

[*Insert sad trombone noise.*]

But you know what? If the resonance of art lies solely in the eye of the beholder, then for me, that kitchen door *was* art. And I *still* remember the way it felt to stand outside the door, head cocked, being transported to an "else"—someplace else, someone else, something else.

That is what we are all hoping for as readers. And just as one woman's kitchen door is another woman's van Gogh, there isn't going to be a uniform response to your writing. I'd venture if you were to ask five people their five favorite books of all time, you'd find little overlap. Subjectivity plays a *huge* part in acquisitions, and I guarantee that even some of the books topping *The New York Times* list right now had folks who couldn't finish the read, because it was just not to their tastes.

That being said, if you get twenty-five to thirty of these types of responses, it may be time to take a closer look at your project for these three telltale "not for me" offenders:

DERIVATIVE WORKS: You often hear agents say to include "comp titles" in your query—books already on the shelves that are comparable to your work—but there's a fine line between *comparable* and *derivative*. For example, a fantasy young adult novel featuring teens pitted against one another, fighting to the death, is ground that's pretty well tread. Whether there's room for one more footprint will depend on whether anything that uniquely resonates can be found in the rest of the narrative.

SECOND-ACT SLUMPS: You have a bang-up opening, but that middle section is a meandering mess that's just keeping the word count up before you get to the fabulous ending. Your B-story line *must* be as high-stakes as your A-story line, and there should never be a sizable section where your writing tries to sustain us without furthering the plot.

QUESTIONABLE CONTENT: I love a good murder mystery, no matter the genre or style. But when there is gratuitous violence (and especially adult perpetrators against kids), it takes a lot of careful handling in terms of execution, originality, and plot necessity for me to be able to get fully behind that kind of narrative.

Other than that, I would say get back into the kitchen and get cooking on another agent sub list! I'll be here at the door, dreamily listening.

Dear FYSA,

I signed with my agent after picking between two offers of representation. Unfortunately, in recent conversations with him I can't help but have the feeling that maybe I chose the wrong one. Can I reach out to the other offering agent and say I'd like to talk again?

Signed,
Regretful Ruby

Dear Regretful,

A few years ago I made an offer on something at the same time as another agent. When the client called to say she was going to sign with the other agent, she actually started crying and said, "I'm probably making a huge mistake." To be honest? *She totally was.*

Kidding! It was disappointing, but the mitigating circumstance that led her to choose the other agent involved something that would've never occurred to me—nor did it ring true for what I felt this publishing path would look like—and that's something to define for yourself *first*: Why did your agent win out over the other, and how has that changed in the time you've been together?

Once you're clear on your own mitigating factors, initiate that conversation … with your *current* agent. Address what you feel has changed and see if there's a solution to be had.

You don't specify whether the agent you signed with has submitted your manuscript yet, but I hope he hasn't, because "my book didn't sell" is way down the list of reasons for seeking new representation. Sometimes books don't sell. And as long as the agent submitted to reputable houses that publish the kind of book you wrote, then your next steps should be about looking forward to what's next—not backward by revisiting the same work with someone new. Signer's Remorse doesn't exist in a vacuum. There's a reason you feel this way, and speaking directly to the source is the best foot forward. Worst-case scenario? Identify an unmalleable aspect of your current agent and do an awkward "I really wanted to take *you* to the Sadie Hawkins dance" call with the other agent. There's no guarantee she'll still be interested, and everyone might feel kinda oogy about the switch, but this is your career—you get to decide who advocates for it.

Dear FYSA,

I am getting a lot of requests to see my full manuscript, but so far the rejections say, "While I love your writing, concept, plot, etc., I have to be 5 bajillion trillion percent in love with a project to take it on."

My question then is: Why don't literary agents act more like Hollywood agents, who may not see you as perfect for a certain role, but believe in your talent and send you on other auditions? Why don't literary agents say, "This project may not be for me, but I see that you can write and are a professional"? Why not invest in the talent and potential for future earnings?

Landing with an agent who happens to fall madly, passionately, absurdly, ludicrously in love with my project sometimes seems as likely as finding a unicorn.

Thanks,
Underappreciated in Arizona

Dear Underappreciated,

This question is so delicious that I printed it out and *ate* it.

You managed to include my favorite percentage, a unicorn reference, *and* a subtle underlying coyness laced with a *soupçon* of *ennui*. It's like I Scott Bakula'd into your body and *wrote this question to myself*. The mention of Hollywood slyly clues the reader in as to the best way for me to frame the response: by performing a one-woman show titled *Bajillion*.

[FADE IN]

INTERNATIONAL LITERARY AGENT OFFICES. DAY.

(Numerous novel covers are framed on the wall and there is a very large bar cart upstage left. Enter BARBARA, a 40-cough-coughcough-year-old agent.)

BARBARA *(on cell phone)*

"You are the best, you are my favorite, I kill for you, I die for you. Now go write! The world is waiting!" *(She hangs up, addresses audience.)* "No idea who that was."

(BARBARA *unbuttons a $1,500 Burberry coat and throws it in the corner. She picks up a crystal decanter from the bar cart, sloshes some liquid into a glass and slugs it. Moving to her desk, she opens her laptop.)*

BARBARA

"Pass, pass, pass, *yawn*, pass, boooring, pass, *yuck*, pass, pass *twice*, pass pa—wait a minute." *(Music swells as she picks up the laptop and holds it adoringly.) "I love you. I love you. I love you* 5 bajillion trillion percent!" *(She kisses laptop passionately. Lights down.)*

[The End]

That, folks, is how you win a Tony.

Totally accurate depiction of how I work. I mean, not the liquor part—who even has time to use a glass anymore?—but the rest is spot on: I *have* to love it. And *you want me to*! Imagine this: You are choosing a nanny for your children and are down to the final two candidates. One nanny says, "Looking for a paycheck, daddy-o, and this will do just fine!" And the other nanny says, "Um, is it me, or are your children *geniuses*? I love them 5 *bajillion trillion percent.*"

I can speak only from my own experience, but if I see something spectacular in the writing but not the project, then I *do* call up the author and howl, "*Yes!* I mean, not *this* plot. Or these characters. Or … any of this. But do you wanna play with me?"

Take, for example, Sarah Nicole Lemon. She attended a *Writer's Digest* webinar I was instructing and submitted a women's fiction partial. I told her, "You are wildly talented, but I think your style is better suited to young adult. If you'd like to write a YA novel, I'll sign you now—because I believe in you that much. You in?" And she was! And I sold it! And more!

I'll have to ding you a little bit on that Hollywood agent comparison, too—because I have a secret past in Hollywood (really), and it's not that different. They might look at skills first and roles second, but you *do* need to blow an agent away for them to sign you. If you take a pie in the face and fall over a potted plant, they don't think, "Well *here's* the guy to play Lieutenant Stoic in the new season of *Cop Drama.*" They ground their choices the same way we literary reps do: in a little bit of industry knowledge and a lot of gut instinct.

Believe it or not, like a sweeping musical score over the credits, our hearts rise and fall with every swell and break right alongside our clients'—so, like you, we have to have some serious love fueling the process. Any artist's advocate would be underserving his clients if he didn't have the same passion to see his people succeed.

All of this is to say: I absolutely hear your frustration—because it is accurate, in a sense, but for all of the right reasons. And what I would also add is that if your main complaint is that your current work is not "lovable" enough, but that you have the kind of talent that can write something that is? *Then write it!* Pen something new, then get out there with another project.

Dear FYSA,

I've revised and edited, researched agents, followed all the guidelines ... and have had no luck! Do you have any super-secret query tips or tricks you could offer me?

Signed,
Luckless in Los Angeles

Dear Luckless,

I have to ask: What does "no luck" mean to you? Here is what I would deem "unlucky," as point of reference in terms of having done everything right but still not placing the work:

- Your query is concise and accurately presents the hook (a log line), the book (four to five lines of *premise*, not *plot*) and the cook (a short bio).
- You have an appropriate understanding of the genre the work embodies, as well as the appropriate word count for that genre.
- You have submitted the query to thirty-plus agents.
- You have had requests for partial and full manuscripts.
- Your rejection letters have been more personal than form letters.
- A particular issue with the manuscript has been echoed by more than one industry professional, such as "too quiet" or "trouble connecting with voice," pointing to a flaw that is structural—not cosmetic.

If these points are ringing true and you still haven't received an offer of representation, it's time to think about what you should be writing next. This may not be what you want to hear, but the truth is, there really is no "trick." But a lot of times that first manuscript needs to sashay out stage left in order for the real blockbuster to break into the spotlight.

Dear FYSA,

If a publisher makes an offer to me directly before I'm agented, how big does it have to be to interest you?

Signed,
Offer-In-Hand

Dear In-Hand,

If you are going to call or email me to loop me in on an offer, you will want to tell me the publishing imprint, the editor, and the details of the offer. (Help yourself out by making sure that the publishing house is reputable, even if an indie imprint.) But really, in order to truly interest me, it has to depend on three factors:

Do I love the book?
Do I love the book?
Do I love the book?

It won't matter if it is $1,500 or $1.5 million if I love the book, because either way I am going to do whatever I can to make sure that it is indeed the *best* offer we can shake out—for the book *and* for your career. There might be further editorial work needed to take it to the next level, or there may be an editor at another house that I know would *love* this book and be willing to throw some serious effort at acquiring and building your career under her imprint instead. Either way, the main factor is that I have to read and connect with the material. Then you put the offer in *my* hand, baton-style, and let me run with it.

Dear FYSA,

I am in a mixed-genre writing group and I write women's fiction. One night, we started talking agent submissions and someone asked me why I would query a male agent when my writing is so female-centric. I wish I could say we all laughed it off, but the conversation then got really intense. I have to admit, it made me wonder—should I focus exclusively on female agents?

Sincerely,
Genre Exclusive

Dear Genre,

Woo boy! That must've been a doozy of a conversation. I hope the pinot flowed as plentifully as the vitriol, and that no one weaponized a pencil.

There is a lot to unpack here—but more so for the individual who suggested that you need a like-gendered agent than for you. The unfortunately prevalent "to really *get* me you have to be just like me" mindset has been the catalyst for about a million years of sociological and anthropological dissonance, am I right? That person must feel so isolated, and has probably missed out on so many amazing books because they didn't feel echoed in their likeness. Being a writer should be like eating at a Vegas buffet—try a little bit of everything! And also, stay hydrated.

In agenting, sure, there is still an element of *getting* you, but that kind of subjectivity is not gender-based. My job is to facilitate a captivating tale—a tale that can be told by someone in a kilt, a skirt, a fine pair of hunting cargos, or no pants at all! None of us has actually ridden a dragon or fought the Socs or caught a Golden Snitch, but we can recognize the human emotion captured within these experiences, and can therefore relate to it. And that is who you should be looking to partner with—someone who finds the relatability in your work and thus foresees how to place it on the shelves.

Devising a list of potential agents to query is about researching within your genre and the broader marketplace to find out who represents the *kind of book* you do. Resources abound on how to go about doing this. Make your list based on an educated look at what else the agent and the agency have ushered through to publication. You and I don't have to look alike, sound alike or vote alike, and only one of us has to bathe consistently. The only thing you really need to have in common with your agent is that *both* of you love your book.

Dear FYSA,

It's very clear that you only sign things that you love. No offense, but why do you think that your taste in literature is the right taste?

Signed,
A Salty Scribe

Dear Salty,

If you had a hype crew behind you right now, they would all put their clenched fists in front of their mouths and go, "Ohhhh!" Then *my* hype crew would aggressively defend me by sneering and crossing their arms in an intimidating pose. But right now one crew member is eating a sandwich and the other is actually just a mop in a bucket, so I guess there will be no dance-off today.

Look: It's a fair question. It's also a nuanced answer, however, because of the words "right" and "taste."

As far as "right"—gosh, I mean okay, I haven't been wrong about anything since June of '98—but there is *no such thing* as "right" taste in literature. To be honest, there are some gigantic, Pulitzer Prize–winning novels that I would've passed on after twenty pages. And as far as "taste," I'd like to think my taste falls under a single umbrella. Not one labeled by genre, or by POV, or even narrative style, but simply under the label: Compelling. I sign things that I find compelling. I would then break down the subgenres under *compelling* as follows:

- Achingly Compelling
- Intriguingly Compelling
- Joyfully Compelling

ACHINGLY COMPELLING: Take D. Watkins and his *New York Times* bestselling memoir, *The Cook Up*, which explores his coming-of-age in East Baltimore. D. has a lyrical bounce to his prose (and the memoir is peppered with slang), and when I read his pages I cried (more than once!) on the A train. I couldn't stop thinking about it. When I called D.—and he can attest to this—I said, "I have no business representing this because it isn't what I excel at placing, but it has changed me on a cellular level and I had to call you and at least try and beg you to let me." In his D. Watkins way, he chuckled and said, "Yeah, let's do this."

INTRIGUINGLY COMPELLING: With Samantha Downing and her psychological-suspense novel *My Lovely Wife*, I could not predict what was going to happen at *any* turn of the page. When I called her to offer representation, I said, "This is wildly disturbing. And I love it. What do you think is *wrong* with us?"

JOYFULLY COMPELLING: Bill Schweigart and I originally connected with his debut *The Beast of Barcroft*, which was the first in a proposed horror series (all three eventually published as The Fatal Folklore trilogy). At one point while reading—*reading!*—a scene that takes place in a basement, something happened and I literally screamed out loud. Again, while on the A train. Then I laughed maniacally that a *sentence* made me do that. *Huh.* Hang on. Now I'm realizing how unhinged I must have appeared to my fellow commuters. No wonder I always get a seat with plenty of room. Anyway! Being taken on a joyride in a novel—whether it be a romance, a thriller, a satire, or a comedy—is just as compelling to me as being caught off guard by a plot twist or connecting to the beats of hope and sorrow in the life story of someone else. Of course, one woman's compelling read might be another woman's snoozefest, but that's why you should be querying all kinds of agents! While I like to tell my spouse that my opinion is the only one that matters, you and I know that isn't true. So get out there and find the advocate that will alienate themselves to an entire uptown train because they found your book to be ... wildly compelling.

Dear FYSA,

Have you ever signed a book that you felt was just the draft of something with the potential to truly be fabulous?

Signed,
Drafty in Detroit

Dear Drafty,

Honestly, *everything* I sign is in draft form. I've yet to ever sign something an editor didn't then make roughly eleven hundred times better. But I think what you are asking about is an honest to goodness *draft*. Look, I love me a good shitty first draft. But have I ever *signed* a shitty first draft because I see the bones of something better? No. But I *have* signed books I knew wouldn't sell (because of genre fatigue or massive similarities to something already out there) because I knew the writer was going to write me something new that *would* sell. And I've seen horrifyingly shitty first drafts from authors I already rep wherein I can see the bones of something stunning. But that's similar to signing clients because I know they have talent, even if I can't sell their first book—they've proven they have the chops to knock it out of the park once they dig in. My advice: Get 50K words of a shitty first draft down in sixty days. Then dig in and make it Shinola.

Dear FYSA,

How do you know when enough is enough when querying agents? Should you ever tell yourself, "Well, you've beaten this idea to death and no one is interested—it's time to move on." Or should you just say, "The hell with giving up. I'm not crazy and have a great idea. I just have to keep trying." (This is my preferred way of thinking.) My feedback is often, "Love your writing, but I'm not sure I could get enough books sold to make it worth my while." Any advice?

Sincerely,
Losing Steam

Dear Steamy,

I will beat an idea to sawdust, pour some water over it, form the sawdust *back* into an idea, and beat it some more—so maybe I'm not the best judge of when to say when (in effort or in gin). But let me try and lay some basic ground rules in thinking here. If we're talking ten rejections, no way. Twenty? Start looking for similar themes in those letters, and apply what you can to your work. If you start knocking on the door of thirty and (this part is key) can't seem to find a common thread of why something isn't working, then it may be time to run out to the mound and take away the ball. During any submission process you should always be working on a new manuscript, so give that one the chin nod and tell him to start warming up his arm.

Again, the key to sustaining a submissions process in the face of rejection is to look for anything you can revise based on the passes you get. If there is nothing concrete to apply, then moving to a new book after a healthy submission round may even help you get a clearer understanding of what wasn't resonating with the first.

The response of "I'm not sure I could get enough books sold to make it worth my while" gives me pause, however. I represent books that I've sold for a rootillion dollars and books I've sold for a wink and a smile, and I feel just as passionate about the ones that garner couch change as I do the ones that make the Prada store manager shiver with pleasure at the mere sight of me. For me (and many other agents I know), "worth my while" boils down to something I would kick myself for not at least *trying* to sell. Which, I now realize, is why my office floor is occasionally covered in sawdust and gin.

The shorthand of all this is to say rejection can cause doubt, but the good news is you're collecting responses, which means your work *is* getting read. It sounds like you're getting feedback that doesn't address the competency of your plotting and/or prose, so I have hope that there will be someone out there who values that and will get you a great deal!

Dear FYSA,

Once you've signed with an agent and are officially on the client list, how should that change an agent's response time to you? My agent has kindly been working with me to revise my manuscript, but each time I resubmit it to her (pulling long hours to turn things around as quickly as possible), I have to wait another four to eight weeks, sometimes longer, for her to review it and get back to me. I had expected things to move along more quickly once I'd made the roster, but perhaps that was naïve. What is reasonable to expect at this stage?

Sincerely,
On the Hook

Dear Hooked,

Hmmm. I hear you. I have a great deal of interest in making sure that my clients understand that when they meet and exceed deadlines, they will get the same from me. Personally, if I don't read and respond within four weeks, I start to feel soul-eatingly bad. And sometimes, that even gets to *six* weeks [dons cone of shame] [faces corner].

However! That is about *me*, not *my ability as an agent to best represent the work*. And so there are rare instances where I will allot more time. Perhaps one of these is true in your case:

1. A SECOND OR THIRD REVISION ON FICTION: When reading a subsequent novel revision, I often need to etch-a-sketch my brain a little before diving in. If I have read and commented on the work and then the author turns the revisions around too quickly, say in a week or two, I need more distance to look at it with fresh eyes. This is especially true for suspense and mystery, or any work where there are clues or twists. If I already know what's coming or whodunit, it can be difficult to evaluate the tension or the effectiveness of the twists in a third revision.

2. ADDITIONAL READS: In an instance like the aforementioned, I may enlist a colleague to read and report back, and I need to respect that reading *my* client's work is not going to occupy positions one through seven on her to-do list.

3. AN OVERLY AMBITIOUS CLIENT ROSTER: There is only one you, whereas your agent has only one set of eyes for an entire client list. I have found that the closer I get to fifty *active* clients, the more I fantasize about cloning. That seems to be the tipping point for me where I can't quite give everyone the attention I pride myself on and things start to get jostled on the to-do list. When I find myself at that point, it's time to take a serious look at my roster and consider how successful I have been as someone's advocate, and whether or not it is time to admit we just aren't getting there with this manuscript or, sad to say, as a team. But there is always a period of time where the pigeon drives the bus before I realize what the issue is, and response time to clients is a big sign.

4. LIFE: I don't have an assistant read things before me, and my workdays are busy, so my reading gets done mostly at night and on the weekends. Now, I'm a wife and a mom, so take those windows of time and throw in someone barfing, a vacation, Aunt Jody's eightieth b-day, someone else barfing, etc., and we bump up against a bit of a delay.

No matter what the issue is, take the responsibility to communicate with your agent. Communication is not only allowable here, it is an integral part of the agent/author relationship. I would *really* hope that any client would think it was fair to give me at least four weeks to respond after submitting a full manuscript, but then at that four week point I wouldn't have a problem getting an email saying, "Hiya! Just curious if you have had a chance to dip in yet?"

Dear FYSA,

While writing my first book, a memoir, I was lucky enough to sign with a prominent agent. Early on, she was extremely helpful with suggestions, but soon after I completed the manuscript, she stopped communicating with me. After months of failed attempts to reestablish a line of communication, I terminated our relationship. I published the book with an indie publisher, and it has sold quite well. Now, I'm completing a second memoir, and again getting ready to contact agents. Should my queries mention that I was previously represented by this agent? Would agents be impressed that she chose to represent me, or wary of the fact that we parted company? What do you recommend?

Sincerely,
Second Time Around

Dear Second-Timer,

I recommend we hang out over mai tais since you have lived enough fabulousness to write not one but *two* memoirs. You must have some pretty great stories to tell. And I like mai tais.

In this instance, however, do mention you were previously represented by Madame Agent, but be sure to specify that it was for another project, so that it's clear that *this* memoir hasn't been shopped around town yet. Indeed, as you postulated, all that you are alluding to here is that a respected name in the business found something in your previous work to be excited about. The circumstances of your relationship and eventual parting aren't as important as the content of the current work you are asking other agents to consider (and those of us in the business know that representation can cease for any number of amicable reasons on both sides of the table). A simple, "I was previously represented by Madame Agent with my debut, but this has not yet been shopped," will suffice.

I want to circle back to something else you mentioned, though: that your debut sold "quite well." What does that mean to you? In some cases, fifteen hundred copies for an indie house is a nice take, but in a larger market it won't fuel your case that there is an audience waiting to hear more from you. If your number is in that ballpark, be prepared with further stats to demonstrate the momentum and demand for a second work. Was it the top-selling nonfiction book on your publisher's list for three months? Did it garner reviews in notable media? Do you have blurbs from respected authors? If you are going to call your previous work a success in your query, make sure it stands up to the accolade.

Dear FYSA,

After submitting to seven imprints, all of whom passed, my agent said she "will no longer be actively submitting" my manuscript and asked what I am working on next. Some of my friends have had agents submit their manuscripts to as many as twenty imprints. Why isn't my agent getting back out there with something she initially said she believed in?

Sincerely,
Short End of Stick

Dear Shorty,

Generally speaking, I usually hit ten to twelve imprints on a first-round submission and hope to make that great sale within those initial connections. But if I feel the work is receiving purely subjective rejections, I'll find further avenues to pursue and gear up for round two. Your agent may have a myriad of reasons on why she feels it is best to look towards "what's next" rather than "who's next." These reasons are up to and including the following:

1. THE ISSUE WITH YOUR PROJECT is a unanimous one (meaning that all seven of those editors replied with some variation of the same concern), and one that isn't easily addressed with further revision. For example: "We already have a sci-fi fantasy featuring ninja mermaids in the queue," or, "The protagonist was unlikable without still being accessible," or, "The story is just too quiet."

2. THE MARKET IS SATURATED with the themes explored in your work and no new angle is being explored in yours.

3. ONLY A FEW IMPRINTS are looking for your type of story or publish it well, and those few imprints are the ones that have passed.

4. THE MARKET HAS CHANGED and the appeal of your subject or even your whole subgenre has waned.

5. THE AGENT HAS A SHARP EYE for which editors want which projects in your subgenre, and/or *only* works in your subgenre and always sells to the same six or eight editors because she feels there isn't anyone else with similar taste.

Or any combination of the above. Or your agent is spending your submission time browsing designer shoes online. (*Holy delicious* do I need to get on the waitlist for the Tory Burch Kingsbridge Mule.)

The fact is, publishing journeys are like fingerprints on a martini glass: They are all different, and—hey, who's been drinking out of my martini? I will grant you this: When your agent said she wouldn't be "actively submitting" further, she should have followed that up with a clear series of supporting reasons why—even if they are hard for you to hear. Remember, your agent *does* believe in the manuscript—she never would have shopped it at all if she didn't—but belief alone doesn't sell books, or my butler would be writing this from my private island.

Sometimes, too, we agents can believe in the *author* a little more than the book, and the idea of the first novel needing to get out of the way to get to the real gold is not a unique one. When I signed Renée Ahdieh, I told her that I was going to go ahead and shop her first young adult manuscript, but that I had a feeling we were going to hear *no*, and I told her why I thought we would hear *no*. I also told her, however, that I had faith that whatever she applied her talents to next would sell. And that's exactly what happened: *The Wrath and the Dawn* was her second effort, and a bestselling one at that. But I was very clear with her from the start about my intent.

Another takeaway here is that if you keep looking to the left and the right, at what other writers' agents are doing, you may fall off the path. You have *your* career and *your* agent, not theirs. Clarify with your agent why she is looking forward to what's next, and thoughtfully consider doing the same.

Dear FYSA,

I received an offer of representation for my young adult novel. When I notified the other agents who had the full manuscript that I was withdrawing from consideration, I got an additional five offers! What would you advise I ask of the offering agents in this situation?

Sincerely,
Full Dance Card

Dear Happy Dancer,

Well, first of all, if I am one of the offering agents, I advise you to pick me. I am *delightful*.

But really, thank you so much for this question, because this happens more often than most authors realize. When multiple agents make an offer on the same manuscript, there are indeed several questions you should ask the offering parties, *and* yourself, in order to determine which one might be your best match. I should note for others here that these questions should *also* be considered even if only one agent is offering. After all, an offer isn't an obligation—it's an invitation, right? So invite them into a conversation!

First, let's assume that each of the offering agents is someone you chose for a particular reason, and not merely the result of a shot of tequila and a handful of darts flung at the pages of the *Guide to Literary Agents.* I would suggest taking a page out of my client Traci Chee's approach when the same thing happened to her—open a new document on your computer or grab a legal pad and write every agent's name and the primary reason why you queried each one at the top.

Next, take a look at how long each agent has been in practice and how many clients he represents. We'll call the resulting comparison *bandwidth versus experience.* A newer agent with only a few years under his belt may have a greater bandwidth for more personal attention and editorial work, while an agent with a robust and lengthy client list has the reputation that accompanies years of experience to guide your career. Which is more important to you? (Hint: There is not a wrong answer here.)

Next, let's take a look at subrights management. How does the agent handle film, foreign, audio, and merchandising rights? There isn't necessarily a "good" versus "bad" way to handle rights, as long as the agent has practices in place in order to take advantage of said rights, as well as examples of previous sales resulting from these practices. Don't merely ask, "Do you think this can sell film and foreign rights?"—because the answer will be an obvious yes. That's a wasted question and you get only three wasted questions before I honk an air horn over the phone line.

Following that, ask what the agent is thinking insofar as the intensity of a round of revisions before shopping to publishers. Again, no wrong answer here, just something for you to compare, and to consider which course you feel resonates as the right next step. You can also ask how many editors she sees herself approaching on an initial round of submissions—but don't ask *which* editors or *which* houses, as you can safely assume if you've done your homework that the agent is not just sending to Bob Snodgrass from Snodgrass Publishing & Hog Feed Inc. (although I heard Bob *was* one of the underbidders on *50 Shades*). That would count as another wasted question, and I would open the drawer with the air horn in it.

Finally, *do* ask to speak to one of the agent's current clients. Let's assume none of the clients are going to be like, "Dude, she day-drinks and keeps calling me Gary. My name is *Renée*." (Geez, Gary, why you trying to play me like that on a referral call?) Ask about turnaround and response times on reads and revisions, about communication styles, and about what, if any, support you can expect from other agency clients and colleagues.

Then ask the client, "What is your favorite thing about working with him, and what is one thing you would change about his representation style if you could?" Now that person might say something that you don't prioritize, which is just as solid an answer as if she'd said something that you *do*. It's a helpful insight into the mechanizations of that agent and her business practices, and when you have fairly evenly qualified candidates vying to be your advocate, every little insight can help.

You can ask anything else you want, of course, but if I may be so bold, I'd like to share something I wrote to a new client of mine whom I acquired in a six agent scrum similar to yours: *This decision most likely will come down to you sitting quietly for a moment and listening to what your instinct is telling you about what you want your partnership to look and* feel *like.*

I truly believe the agent/author relationship is a unique one, and there will almost inevitably be a lot of swells and buckles along the way. No single publishing path is the same—it may take months, even *years* to sell your book, and the sale is only the ship leaving the dock. There is a long journey ahead. Find someone you can stand strong with, whether lashed to the ballast in a storm or gliding in calm waters with both of your faces tilted up to the sun, thinking, *What a ride.*

PART 3

Working With an Editor and Publisher

So! You have a book deal! Congrats! Wow, that day your agent called you to tell you that your book will be published ... there really isn't anything like it. It's your birthday and Arbor Day and bottomless Bloody Mary brunch all at once! Then you have the phone call with the editor—and it. Gets. Even. *Better.*

They love the book. It's the best thing they've read all year. They cannot believe your talent—it's otherworldly! Everyone is so excited to have you on the list. Because you are a genius. Every day of your life is 78 degrees and sunny with a mild breeze from here on out!

And then you get your first editorial letter.

It's nineteen pages long. And the manuscript is marked up. On. Every. Page. And at one point the editor just scrawled "meh" with an arrow pointing to a bracket with the confession scene.

They hate you. They hate the book. The editor made a terrible mistake and they have had several meetings about how awful your book really is and what kind of day-drinking nonsense led to them to offer you a contract. Every day is 42 degrees and drizzly with a wind from the Northeast.

But you dig in. Because you are no longer *writing* a novel you are *publishing* a novel. You work for six weeks on your edits.

You ignored your children. You forgot your anniversary. You bled your prose, you murdered your darlings, you slaughtered the weird dinner party scene that you now can totally agree was an anchor dragging down your intended pacing. And you know, that now, this manuscript is perfect. It was all worth it. You didn't think you had it in you but now, *now*, this is the manuscript of your editor's dreams. You did everything that was asked of you and *more*. You click send. You take a shower and buy your spouse some flowers and take the kids to the park.

And six weeks later your editor sends the manuscript back for "one more round to really clarify the backstory of the mother" and to "do another clean up on some of the more redundant phrasing." And there it is again, that "meh."

And you find yourself fully clothed in the bathtub rocking back and forth humming "This little light of mine …" over and over.

You, my friend, are in a totally typical publishing cycle. One that needs to be navigated with as much humor as intensity. Because now? Now the real work begins.

Dear FYSA,

What does an agent's pitch of my book to an editor look like? Is it a formal submission package, just as I'd send to an agent, or do agents personalize their pitches in ways that writers never could? For instance, do they ever say things like, "I really think this book has breakout potential," or anything else that subjective?

Sincerely,
Pitch Perfect

Dear Pitch Perfect,

Well, personally, I always like to open my pitches with a joke, and then with the age and weight of the author. So basically, it goes like this:

Editor: Hello, Johnson speaking.

Me: Barbara Poelle here. Didja hear the one about the peanut butter on toast? Well, I'm not gonna tell you 'cause I wouldn't want you to spread it! Ha! So I have a book by a fifty-six-year-old man who weighs 175 pounds …

Wait, I left out the part where I make a honky horn sound at the punch line of the joke. But you folks are a smart lot—you probably inferred it.

Okay, okay. For realsies, I pitch in different ways (phone, email, in person over drinks, at a conference) to different editors for a variety of reasons, but I would safely say that I use lines directly from the author's original query 90 percent of the time, in both fiction and nonfiction. But I always add my own personal touches as you alluded to in your question. For example, in my pitch, I might compare a client's novel to a novel the editor and I had success with in the past. Or I might talk about how I felt reading this if it paralleled how it felt to read one of my previous bestsellers—that very specific barometer that told me I needed to sign the client and get it in front of that editor at that imprint. Or for a nonfiction proposal I am shopping, I might highlight recent nonfiction comp titles that have done well that this new voice and proposal builds on. (As for the novels and proposals themselves, the author and I would have already discussed revisions before shopping, and any that the author agreed with would be applied to the material. I do not go in and "personalize" anything in a novel or proposal.)

Regardless, 99.9 percent of the time, because of my reputation and the subject matter which is clearly in their imprint's wheelhouse, whether fiction or nonfiction, the editor is going to ask to see the material. Then, for fiction, I send along my written pitch and attach the entire novel to the email, and for nonfiction I send my pitch and attach a proposal.

I still do enjoy calling editors for the initial pitch, and in that case it's all me. I want the editor to hear how excited and certain I am that this book is the next big thing. I only have their full attention for a minute, so I will provide a truncated pitch with a bit of zazzle, like, "You know the guy right before the guy who is the millionth customer? That is how you are gonna feel if you don't read this *tonight*, 'cause it's gonna happen, and it's gonna happen big." And then I do the honky horn sound.

Dear FYSA,

When a contract is negotiated, what are the main points an author should be aware of? What is that process like?

Sincerely,
How's It Look

Dear Howie,

After your verbal deal is made with an editor, the editor and I agree on the basic terms at point of sale and then the editor generates and sends me a "deal memo." I either contest or approve the points in the deal memo, and then when it reflects what we both agree are the terms at point of sale, the editor sends that along to her contracts department at the publishing house.

What transpires next ... hmm ... well, have you ever heard of the ancient Roman punishment poena cullei? Well, think of the process as "Poellea Cullei." Similar in concept, but in this case, the opposing contracts manager and I are sewn into a sack, which is then filled with precedent, legalese, and rapid-fire emails (which increase in scoff and incredulity simultaneously) and thrown into a river.

A typical publishing contract runs upward of twenty pages of eye-crossing legalese and worst case scenario outlines. The good news is I have the agency boilerplate as a starting point. The "boilerplate" refers to the contract clauses that have been tirelessly hammered and thus previously established specifically by my agency that allow us for short cuts on newer contracts, because I don't have to go back and reestablish that language. I already have my preferred language in many of the major clauses, (but every contract I push a little harder to establish further precedent and better terms where I can).

Additionally, my agency has a contracts consultant who previously worked in a big five publishing house for years, so I get to run alllll kinds of legalese and clause language by her and use her powers for good.

Insofar as to what you as the author want to pay attention to, and how much you want to invest understanding every clause, well that is totally up to you! I have clients (some of whom are lawyers themselves!) who tell me, "Looks great, thanks." And I have clients who chose to hire an additional outside lawyer to take a look at the contract simultaneously as I do with my consultant. Life Hack!: If you do go with an outside lawyer, make sure they are well versed in *publishing* contracts. Your brother-in-law the divorce lawyer isn't going to know that the U.K. royalty percentages are off, or what the threshold for high discount should be. (I don't know if that actually constitutes as a "life hack" but I like to picture myself appearing in a small cartoon burst in your mind wearing a helmet and holding a mallet and saying "Life Hack!" and I. Look. Adorable.)

If you decide to let your agent and their contracts person run the show for you, the points I always tell my clients to eyeball are the delivery dates, the wording of the "morality clause" (which allows the house to cancel a novel should the behavior of the author directly and clearly negatively impact the sale of the book to the intended audience) and the option clause.

The delivery dates need to reflect your true assessment of when you can turn in your book(s). Make sure they are doable. The morality clause? Look, if your book is based on your "No Make-Up Face Over 40" Instagram, and you are actually secretly spackling on the Mary Kay before all of those selfies, it's gonna hurt all of us. Similarly, if you are secretly a horrible Twitter troll who can't help but heap online abuse on everyone's feed, this is also going to potentially damage your book deal. And also ... just ... stop doing that. Finally, the option language should be comfortably restricted should you have other genres you would like to pursue, but you and your agent should have discussed this previously.

But let's be honest, you are all flipping to the advance clause first. Look at those zeroes. You did it. You are getting paid to write a book.

Dear FYSA,

What's the best deal in terms of money that a first-time writer can realistically expect to get?

Sincerely,
Cash Curious

Dear Cash Curious,

This one time on a lush, fall day on the University of Minnesota campus, the kind of day that smells like ginger and wood smoke, I was walking to my dorm and a squirrel *fell out of the sky* and hit the ground in front of me.

Have you ever heard of that happening? I actually cried out, "Oh my *God*—are you okay?" and he kind of rolled over and then blasted back up the tree.

That has nothing to do with your question, but I've been wanting, for *years*, to tell someone that happened. I saw a *squirrel fall out of the sky.*

And the wildest part? If I would have been seven seconds faster leaving Econ, it would have *landed on me.* And that, my friends, would be someone else's greatest story of all time. They would still be telling that story in bars. "Keith, tell them about that chick and the squirrel." And Keith would nail the telling of it every time, because that story basically tells itself.

Oh, but you? Anywhere from $1,500 to $1.5 million. So, you know, plan accordingly.

Dear FYSA,

My agent just sold my novel to Ballantine Bantam Dell in a six-figure deal—I am totally overjoyed! My Critique Partner asked if that was enough to quit my day job and it gave me pause—so I thought I would ask—what is the amount that you advise authors to quit their day jobs?

Sincerely,
Hip Hip Hooray

Dear Hipster,

Huge congratulations! And ahhh yes, those days are my favorite days, when I get to call the client and say "BBD is offering 100,000 bags of birdseed to publish your book!"

Hmm?

Oh. Yes, that is correct. For six figure plus amounts I usually say "bags of birdseed" or "bundles of sticks" or "pictures of Neil Patrick Harris" because I have found that once an author hears "-dred thousand dollars" on offer for their book, a wave of white noise descends upon them and they are not able to retain any more information today. And what happens next is what is happening next—someone asks them if they are quitting their day job. So then they will ask me if they should quit their day job. And I will take all of my industry experience and savvy and pointedly and knowingly say, "That is literally none of my business." Because I facilitate their literary career, not their bank account. As long as they deliver quality works and deliver them on time, what they do with the rest of their day is up to them and those who depend on them. But look, maybe 100,000 bags of birdseed *is* enough for you to quit your day job! Let's have Siri do the math—mostly because I have mine set to the Australian dude's voice so I can pretend I am having meaningful discourse with Chris Hemsworth. Ahem. "Chris? Can you math us out on a $100,000 book advance?"

Right then. In broadest possible terms, most six-figure publishing contracts are going to be for initial format as hardcover, and thus will most likely have payment in fourths. That means $25K at initial signing of contract, $25K at delivery and acceptance of manuscript, $25K at initial publication in hardcover, $25K at initial publication in secondary format (trade paperback or mass market paperback).

"Thanks!" Ah I could listen to th–

But it isn't actually $25K in fourths.

"What's that Hemsy?"

It's $25K gross. So accounting for agent commissions, it is actually four payments of $21,250.

"Ah, right, thanks handso–"

Before taxes.

"Pardon me, Christopher?"

That $21,250 is before taxes. So your Uncle Sam is coming with his hand out for up to 35 percent depending on your tax bracket, so you should set aside up to $6K of each of those checks for quarterly payments.

"Yes, well, uh, right, thank yo–"

And let's not forget these four payments are doled out over a period of 18–24 months.

"Yes, THANK you Ch–"

It most likely takes 6–8 weeks for the signing payment, then another 6–8 MONTHS for delivery and acceptance payment. Then another 8–10 months for initial publication. Then a year after that for additional format.

"YESYESTHANKYOUYOUMAYGONOW."

Ahem. Anyway, as you can see, a six-figure advance isn't a six-figure payday. And we use the term advance literally—it is an advance paid to you with an understanding that we all believe, based in part on a P&L (Profit and Loss) compiled by the publisher that your book will sell enough copies to "earn out" this advance. The P&L consists of a multifaceted look at a variety of things, like the performance of previous comp titles, the guesstimated marketing budget, the current market climate, printing and shipping costs, and chicken bones and a lock of hair from Lou Diamond Philips. No, for real, a P&L is like three-fourths math and one-fourth utter nonsense. But it is the most important tool a publisher has when preparing an offer. We all want you to earn out that advance. When you earn out the advance you move to royalty payments that are generally paid out twice a year. But, let's say you do not earn out that $100K, your agent is going to have an uphill climb to get you the same number—or even close to that same number—on your re-up for the next book.

I know, it's … a lot, because suddenly it seems like so … little. This is the reality. It is one that takes financial planning as well as creative energy. And thus, while I can give you a full look at what an advance means and how it is paid out, I simply cannot advise anyone on the threshold that allows them to step back from their day job. Only you can decide when/if the scales tip enough to allow you to be a full-time writer.

Sigh. I know. When we feel like this there is only one thing to do, really … ahem …

"Chris? Please play the fight scene in *Thor: Ragnarok* … in slow-mo … on repeat. Thank you."

Dear FYSA,

My agent just sold my novel in a two-book deal—yay! Here's the thing: This has always been a dream of mine, and my advance is very healthy, but, I love my other career—my "day job" as it were.

But I am worried that will make it look like I am not serious about this. Tell me the behind-the-curtain truth: Will I be taken as seriously as an author by my agent and publisher if I keep my day job?

Sincerely,
Working 9 to 5 to 9

Dear Niner,

Huh, I think I was just talking to your friend. She had the same question, but in an upside down-y kind of way. But hey, welcome to living the dream! And I don't mean your publishing contract, (although congrats!) I mean the slim percentage of folks who *adore* what they do for work. Living in that impossible Venn diagram collision of vocation meeting passion meeting occupation is not something everyone can claim, but when we can, it literally makes everything better. You are preaching to the choir—even if I won the Mega Millions tomorrow I would still be here in the office the day after representing my clients (okay, maybe the day after the day after, because, *champagne*).

And quite frankly whether you are spending your days working in animal husbandry or repurposing driftwood, it's not really any of our concern. The one caveat to any of this is, of course, the difference between writing and publishing. Previously you were writing a novel. Now you are publishing novels. Which means there are edits and revisions and publicity and marketing requirements and a *second* book to write ... under a deadline. But the short answer? Yes, you are taken seriously even if you keep your day job. I have many clients who do so and they find balance. And if you are delivering your manuscripts on time and available for your contractually obligated publicity and marketing appearances, keep that Venn Zen going. It deserves to be honored for the rarity it is.

Dear FYSA,

I'm a member of a writing group in which we're all at varying points in our careers, but we all agree on one fundamental publishing truth: The size of an advance directly dictates the amount of publicity and marketing a book gets, without exception. So, if you're not selling your books for six figures each, are you going to be lost in the swell?

Yours,
Wary in Wisconsin

Dear Wary,

Sure, there are books that are "anointed"—ones that are called a lead title and will have the lion's share of attention in-house. That said, I've seen so many exceptions to this statement that I actually chuckled out loud at your question. Yes, if your book is bought in a five-house auction for seven figures, you can be fairly confident that you'll have the full attention of the publicity and marketing team. But I've sold books for ... wait for it ... *four* figures that had the entire force of those teams at their back—books that went on to become bestsellers. Inversely, I've sold books with many zeroes attached to their advance that then seemed to shimmer and vanish in the eyes (and efforts) of the marketing team. In fact, sometimes the publicity and marketing team has no idea what was paid out in an advance.

There are oodles of ingredients in the Poelle secret sauce that can help with this in a specific, case-by-case basis, but rest assured: Just because you aren't getting six figures up front doesn't mean you won't be getting a six-figure push from behind.

Dear FYSA,

The word lengths for book genres seem so arbitrary. How did publishers arrive at these numbers, what's the sweet spot, and are there ever any exceptions?

Yours,
Count Me In

Dear Count Me In,

Oh my gosh, well—it is *so* fun! Every four years on the twenty-ninth of February, we all get together in a big field, Woodstock style, and tack giant felt targets with numbers on them onto huge bales of hay. Then, designated by genre, we have Velcro suit-wearing human javelins hurl themselves down a muddy runway toward a springboard, and *whammo*! Whatever number they stick to is yelled out, the Genre Keeper writes it on a big board, and we all chant, "Thus has it flown, thus it is known!" Ta-da! *Word counts for the next four years!*

I want that to be true so badly that I just stopped typing to mentally pack a picnic cooler for the event.

Okay, the real answer? Math.

I know. Makes you want the human javelins back, doesn't it?

Agents have nothing to do with word count designations. Publishers arrive at these numbers the same way they do most things: profit and loss statements (Come'ere Lou Diamond Philips. What? No, I do not have scissors behind my back.)

Because books today need to compete more vigorously for people's time and entertainment dollars, publishers are looking at any format, even higher-margin hardcovers, and thinking, *This thing is six hundred pages and looks thick—will that discourage people from even picking it up? Or is that something this genre seems able to support in this market because titles A, B, and C already proved that?* As an agent, therefore, the only reason I make a decision to reject a query based on word count is when the count is impossibly low or impossibly high, rendering the book unpublishable in any P&L. If books were selling at $39.95, we would have much more wiggle room. But think about the price point you buy books at, or would be willing to repeatedly buy books at. Even your personal-household P&L reflects this, right?

And I would say that within any genre, from young adult to adult, we can play with javelins a *liiiittle* bit. You're at least getting the arrow to hit the target at 65K–110K words across the board. As we move into specific genres and subgenres, that's when the true bull's-eye gets defined. But if your pacing is tight and each moment counts, your editor is not going to ding you for a book that is 115K if it feels like 90K.

Dear FYSA,

I'm published in fiction but decided to blog daily through a free online magazine. In the first month, I'm averaging twenty thousand readers a week. What number will help my editor show her publisher there is an audience here for a nonfiction book?

Sincerely,
By the Numbers

Dear By the Numbers,

The conventional wisdom in publishing used to be that we could count on about 10 percent of your regular online readers/followers to buy a book from you, but that has shifted because we (and I personally) have seen folks with online audiences of tens of thousands sell fewer than three thousand copies of a book.

The good news is that publishers know a sizable online following certainly moves the needle, and thus it is always a huge one in the plus column. There just isn't an algorithm we can use to tell what quantity of followers demonstrates a demand for a book. In your case, I like the number twenty thousand. But are those readers willing to graduate to the next level of fandom? They might read your tweets, affirmations, blogs, and Tumblr for free, but would they take out their wallets to see what else you have to say on the subject? The real test of the equation is your approach to your subject matter, and your personal voice, and so you and your editor should work on a proposal that shows *that* as well.

Dear FYSA,

I got my first editorial letter for my debut and all I can say is that I went in the bathroom at work and cried. It was, like, seventeen pages long and basically said every aspect of my novel needed work. Is this normal? I feel like my editor is now regretting buying my book!

Sincerely,
Hiding in the Bathroom

Dear Hiding,

Pretend one of us has a secret history in stand-up comedy. Pretend that in a very early comedy competition in our careers, the three judges sat there completely stone faced while we crushed our best stuff. I mean total A-game. The one about the hunters, the one about the walk of shame from the 7-Eleven, the one about the Denny's bathroom!!! And ... nothing. Not even a dry cough. Now pretend we went off stage and to the bathroom where we screamed into a roll of paper towels. Then we came back out and soon we were informed that we *won*.

And we were elated! And ... baffled. And *angry*. So angry. Why would they put us through that? How did they even decide we won without even a chortle? A guffaw? A smirk? Why did they act like they didn't even *like* us, much less love us?

Until later, in casual conversation with some of the more seasoned comics, we realized, those judges? They were *at work*. They already knew we were funny, or we wouldn't be there. But now they had to take a look all aspects of why they liked us in the first place, and find and make comments about where we could improve. Because they *want* us to be better, and they want to use what they know to make us better.

This is what your editor is doing—she already loves your book. She wouldn't have bought it for the imprint if she didn't. It's not like an editor reads, yawns, stretches, and then reaches for the company checkbook.

Do you know how hard an editor has to fight just to *get* to buy a book? Let me give you a quick look at the process: He reads it, he has to take it to editorial board, get support, maybe a few more reads, then pitch to acquisitions, get the whole team on board, run a P&L, then call me knowing I am going to say "Awww, that's adorable. Call me back when you have a *real* offer." And then he has to start the P&L process all over again and sometimes beg and plead the publisher or CEO and explain *again* why he loves this book. And by then I may have other interest and may be setting up an auction and he has to eat antacids for three days, making bids, until he finally finds out he won the book! And then, he reads it again. And probably again. Before starting your editorial letter.

He already loves your book, but now he is at work. He bought the book because it is very, *very* good. And it is his job to help you make it even better. Your seventeen pages of notes is proof that you won—now get to work because he's making sure that you win with the audience as well.

Dear FYSA,

I have been through two rounds of edits on my novel, and my editor said it is heading to copy edits and I can only make "slight changes here and there" now ... is that all I get? I still feel like there is work to do!

Signed,
Panicky Pen

Dear Pen,

Whenever Husband does home improvement work, I always get the broom and prop it near the doorway in whatever room he is in, because I am sure that he is going to electrocute himself and I'll have to knock him off the current with the wooden broomstick.

Editors have to have a proverbial broomstick with their authors, because all of you would tweak yourself to death. There is always one more edit to make, one more comma to move with ya'll. This is why you have a few structural rounds, a cosmetic round or two and then *thwack*! They knock you off the book and send it to the printers.

Generally speaking, if your book was home improvement, it will look like this:

1. **EDITORIAL LETTER—STRUCTURAL.** Expect entire characters and/or sections to be reworked or even excised. You will have four to six weeks for this.
2. **SECOND ROUND OF REVISIONS—WIRING.** Expect to still have to go deeper on a plot line or character motivation, but only by adding a line or two. Making sure connections in plot and character are clear. One to three weeks.
3. **FIRST PASS PAGES—INTERIOR DESIGN.** A copy editor (CE) is assigned and a master copy is made and this is the only copy you

will work on from here on out. And from here on out will be cosmetic, *not* structural changes. You will be given the opportunity to approve or STET (keep as it) any suggestions made by the CE. One to two weeks.

4. **PAGE PROOFS—KNICK KNACKS.** Make *light* changes to the work. One week.
5. **GALLEYS—"THAT IS NOT THE PAINT COLOR I CHOSE."** Relax, galleys are made from first pass pages, they won't have the tweaks you made in the page proofs. But it kinda looks like a book now, it's getting very exciting.
6. **SECOND PASS PAGES—"OH PHEW, THAT IS THE PAINT; THE LIGHT IN THE ROOM WAS JUST DIFFERENT."** This is the very last time to make any *light* tweaks.
7. **TIME TO SEND TO PRODUCTION**—*Thwack!* Broomstick.

Dear FYSA,

Is it ever okay for a first-time author to request the power to veto a book cover from the publisher? I'm primarily concerned about multicultural books with covers that lighten the skin color of main characters or use silhouettes, cartoonish figures, abstract illustrations, etc.

Sincerely,
Cover Concerned

Dear Concerned,

A few years ago, Husband took me on a pricey bay cruise in San Francisco. While he left to get us some champagne, I managed to sashay into the captain's deck and talk him into letting me drive for a quick minute. (I could talk a fish into wearing pants, people.) Thirty seconds later, lots of ladies in dresses and gents trying to impress them were being tossed hither and thither, and the captain gently but firmly reclaimed the wheel.

Now, obviously in my mind I thought I knew what I was doing. Just pick a point on the horizon and go, right? All of the folks screaming begged to differ.

And that is why we leave certain things to the professionals.

Any good agent will negotiate your publishing contract to allow for client "consultation" on a cover at the very least, and "mutually approval" in the best (rare) cases, because no one wants an author to hate her cover.

Expanding this to concerns regarding multicultural books and the assurance that a protagonist's ethnicity will be reflected properly in the cover art, I wholeheartedly agree, and I will make sure that the editor and publisher do as well.

Most important, keep in mind that covers are trend-based and trends are cyclical, so sometimes the choice to do an illustrated cover, for example, isn't about avoiding an accurate representation so much as it is simply a market decision. Not to mention, some accounts will take *more* copies of a specific book if it hits certain requirements and aesthetics because data shows their customers will *buy* more based on such data and aesthetics, like I have seen many times in craft books and romances.

But no matter what, as a basic rule, it just isn't in the author's best interest to have "veto power" over a cover, especially for a debut. Otherwise you can end up with a whole boatload of crabby folks who have pinot noir Jackson Pollocked all over their clothes.

Dear FYSA,

What's a publisher's stance on authors who wish to use pen names in an age when we are expected to actively promote our work online and off?

Sincerely,
Pseudonymous

Dear Pseudonymous,

Well, as long as you don't choose the name "Engelbert Humperdinck," "Edward Snowden," or "Cher," I don't see why anyone would have a problem with it as long as you do all of your promotion under that name. So if Bob Smith wants to write as Flart Sugarknees, Bob should understand that the publisher may ask for him to have Flart's website, Twitter handle, and Facebook fan page ready to rock, and that he will make all appearances as best-selling author Flart Sugarknees.

And if there are larger concerns about the identity of the author, like if Bob is department head of Sanskrit Studies at Alaska University and doesn't want his colleagues to know he writes werewolf-dolphin erotica, there are other ways to layer an identity to keep his academic work and romance publishing from crossing streams. Or flippers. So essentially, as long as the author is able to fully conduct publishing business under the pen name, it doesn't make a difference if he has one. But don't choose "Poelle." We have all had enough of those.

Dear FYSA,

I submitted my novel directly to a number of publishers. I got one response stating that the publisher was interested only in my e-book rights. The response also stated that I would be liable to pay a $.04 per word "editing charge" if "they" determined that the manuscript needed editing. Are these things normal, or was I dealing with a vanity publisher or scam?

Thanks,
Non-Vanity Writer

Dear Anti-Vanity,

When I was young, I had an "offer to publish" a short story I'd written. It would become part of an anthology as long as I sent a small amount of money in order to "cover binding costs." When I, bursting with pride, brought the letter to my parents, they said, "Oh honey, this is a vanity publisher," and insisted I turn down the opportunity. Oh, how I cried. I cursed! I rode my pink Huffy (named "Sweet Thunder") around and around the block thinking, "Well, my blossoming career is over. At eleven."

But then, oh joy! About a week later I received a legit offer from a magazine you have actually heard of, and that short story thrust me into the spotlight in which I continue to bask today. (The twenty bucks I was paid bought some nice new streamers for Sweet Thunder's handlebars, too.)

Despite the fluctuating tectonics of publishing, there should never be a situation where you are paying a traditional publisher (or agent, remember!) a *dime* up front—the publisher pays editors directly to edit your novel.

On a separate note, however, as far as a publisher being interested in only e-rights, that is certainly plausible, especially if that is the format it specializes in. True, many publishers would want to hang on to print rights, but e-only deals from small publishers are not unheard of, and in fact can be anything from a foot in the door to a competition crusher. So that in and of itself is not a red flag, though of course you need to ask yourself if that is the format you see yourself in.

When in doubt about a particular publisher, the best course is to reach out to other authors published by the imprint and inquire about their experiences. And if you find out the publisher is less than legit? Sweet Thunder has a banana seat—plenty of room for me to take you around the block a few times until the right deal comes along.

Dear FYSA,

As a rather strict grammarian, I am explicit in my use of language, the placement of modifiers in particular. (Speaking French, German, and Latin tends to do that to one.) I've been horrified by the painfully low level of English language standards displayed in books published over the past twenty or so years. This trend has resulted in prose that is painfully dull, illogically [dis-]organized, and flat-footedly pedestrian.

Is there a way of making it plain to the publisher's editors that grammatical and syntactical issues are areas of my own expertise and specific style? Is there a way of imparting that I will not abide anyone's slaughtering my adverbs with pitifully ungrammatical, and illogical, misplacement?

Sincerely,
Grammatically Precise

Dear Precise,

Ugh. Drunken grammar. Sloppy syntax. Participles dangling like the corpses of so many broken piñatas.

That's how I would describe my own writing.

Further, I'm always in such a hurry that I sometimes forget to do a little thing called proofread. I've been known to fire off emails that include such spectacular phrases as, "Can you poop over those net figures to me by end of day?" and "Sorry! You are correct, I had this under the wrong labia in my e-files."

Thus, I sit on this side of the table, and leave the heavy lifting to the professionals. And so do many writers. I can tell you that by and large my clients are satisfied with the edits and revisions suggested; the rare occasion when we need to throw down is rarely about a misappropriated semicolon.

Frankly, unless your last name is *The Chicago Manual of Style*, I would initially give the editor the benefit and courtesy of assuming they have your same skill level of deploying the English language. At the time that you sign with an agent, however, you might want to share with him your concerns so that at point of sale he might mention, "Oh, and this author is basically the love child of Lynne Truss and Billy Strunk, so make sure you are Johnny-on-the-Spot with the mechanics of the edits."

Then they'll have fair warning if you decide to load a T-shirt gun with "STET" and blast away when you receive your copy edits. Because rest assured that, as with the content of your work, the grammatical edits being made are *suggestions* to improve the writing, and you and your agent will have ample opportunity to review and address them before publication.

Dear FYSA,

Back in January, a literary review accepted two of my poems. But many months later I've yet to hear when they'll be published. I've reached out to the editors once, just to make sure they received the requested audio recording of the poems (which they responded to more than a month later). I admit—I'm getting antsy. Is it a bad sign that they haven't gotten in contact with me? Or is that normal? Would it be bad form to email them again?

Yours,
Calendar Girl

Dear Calendar Girl,

This question is important because I think it speaks to a larger publishing industry (and societal) issue: *ghosting*. The term refers to the abrupt severing of contact with someone without explanation—

a practice made all too easy by a twenty-first-century communication shift to email and text messaging.

Ghosting is most often used in the context of dating, but a lot of similarities can be drawn between dating and the submission process. (You know, the crushing rejection, the rapid cycling through the five stages of grief, the drinking ...) Even from where I sit, ghosting plays a pernicious and aggravating part in some of my business exchanges. At the very least it's annoying, at the most it's downright disrespectful, and it's *always* disorienting.

Personally, I tend to go from, *Well, maybe they didn't get the email*, to, *Don't you know who I think I am?*, very quickly, and I don't see any reason why you can't do the same ... though maybe with a little less garbage can kicking. (Take my word for it: Although highly satisfying in the moment, the cleanup is *super* boring.)

First, double-check whether there is any previous information on how and when you will be contacted buried in your previous email exchanges. Many publications, for instance, have an auto-response set up confirming receipt of submissions and giving further instructions. (Don't discard these.) You got beyond the auto-response in your case: Be sure you didn't overlook some key as to timing or method of future contact.

If that doesn't resolve it, don't hesitate to drop them another email: "Hello, I wanted to circle back to confirm as previously discussed ..." If there is no answer within seventy-two hours, I'd send an additional email that reads, "Hello, I'm concerned these emails aren't going through. May I have confirmation of receipt?"

Still no answer? Phone call. If you get voicemail: "Hi, this is Calendar Girl. After receiving word of acceptance on my poems several months ago, and sending several emails, I have yet to be contacted regarding next steps. As I am sure you can imagine, this is disorienting. May I please hear from you? My email and phone number are …"

Firm but necessary emails and phone calls shouldn't prevent someone from loving your poetry enough to publish it. But here is what I will say: If you ever feel like the endeavor has become fruitless, draft a final email saying, "If I haven't heard from you by Friday I will assume you are no longer interested in publication and that I am free to submit elsewhere." And then do it—submit those poems elsewhere. Again, as in dating, there are plenty of other garbage cans to kick … I mean, fish in the sea.

Dear FYSA,

My agent sold my young adult novel in a two-book deal to be published next year (yay!). The editor who bought the book then moved to another publishing house, and I was reassigned a new editor. Then that *editor left publishing, and I've yet again been shuffled. I'm feeling adrift. Should my agent be doing something?*

Sincerely,
Anchorless

Dear Anchorless,

Yes. Your agent should do what I do: Have the acquiring editor sign a document, in blood, that completely rescinds their free will and stipulates they will never leave their imprint—*nay, their desk!*—for the duration of your contract.

Hmm? What now? Oh, it turns out I *don't* do that. Because that is not a thing.

What *is* a thing: publishing folks changing jobs, all the time. Sure, that can feel disorienting and disruptive when it happens once—much less twice—in the life span of a single title. (Looking at you M.K. England! But *The Disasters* was anything but!) The good news is that because this situation is relatively common, there *are* practices in place for when an editor leaves a position—and your agent can be instrumental in facilitating them.

The game plan kicks off as soon as the exiting editor calls me and informs me she's leaving. At that point, and this is 100 percent of the time, I let loose with lazy words right into the phone. Even to me, it's upsetting to hear an editor is leaving a project behind in a move. After all, this is the editor who acquired my client because they had the passion and enthusiasm we were looking for—they genuinely *loved* the book. But there's no use boo-hooing things you can't change, so I move on to the next big question: Has a new editor been discussed to inherit the manuscript, and do I think they're a good match?

If so, then sally forth! If not? I will speak to the editorial director or publisher and request a different editor and explain the logic behind my request. (Reasons can range from my perception of personalities to concerns regarding their workload to the overall track record of the inheriting editor.) I will talk to the editorial director or publisher *regardless* during this transition, to discuss what expectations we have insofar as what was already discussed in editorial timeline, marketing and publicity opportunities, etc. Next, I will call the client and break the news that their editor is leaving. And they will shout several lazy words. But then I will inform them of the new editor and why this individual is the right choice for the project, after which said new editor will introduce himself and connect with my client on a phone call, and away we go.

The best thing to remember in all of this is that the original editor, no matter how passionate and enthusiastic, didn't buy your book in a vacuum. She had to compel other editors to read it, pitch it at acquisitions, and basically make the case for why this book was right for the *imprint* as a whole. Then, after the sale, the editor pitches the book to sales and talks it up in marketing meetings—meaning the team is not only already aware of your book, but has been privy to its journey thus far. Yours wasn't the beloved manuscript of a single person, but you were the universal pick of *an entire team* who felt you deserved a seat at their table. Still, I get it. Having an editor leave on your debut publishing venture is unmooring during an already tumultuous time. Just stay the course, trust the process ... and use as many lazy words as needed.

Dear FYSA,

The last several months have been a flurry of revisions, first pass, second pass, and now I do ... what? My book doesn't publish for another six months—what am I supposed to be doing with myself?

Signed,
Twiddling My Thumbs

Dear Twiddle,

Husband once said "a bored Barbara is a dangerous Barbara" so I can totally relate. If I don't have something to accomplish or achieve I am likely to *find* something to accomplish or achieve including captaining a party yacht or challenging someone to a chug-off for a hundred bucks ... against Husband. But you? You simply cannot find time to be bored, because right now you are making spreadsheets of any and every avenue of publicity and marketing that *you* can bring to the table when your publicist is assigned. Spreadsheets will include categories like:

1. Wish list authors to blurb your book.
2. Authors you have relationships with.
3. Local bookstores within a day's driving distance, both independent and chain.

4. Places to have a book launch.
5. Cities with relationships to the author or a character in the book.
6. Local publications and/or media.
7. National publications and/or media that have a direct correlation/relationship with the author, themes, or characters in the book.
8. Possible social media connections with taste makers, acquaintances outside of publishing who have a following that will promote during pub week.
9. Wish list advertising.
10. Wish list media.

Also you should be designing newsletter, a website, securing an author photo, taking time to observe and expand your social media platforms, and tapping into organizations with personal relationships—i.e. a fraternity newsletter, a high school alumni mailing, etc. for publication announcements or ads. Also, how many words a day are you writing of your next book? Because writers write. *So* you best be writing. See? You don't even have time to think about being bored … in fact I've got a hundred bucks that says you can think of five authors to blurb you before Husband chugs this beer. Ready? [*"Wait, babe, what?"*] Go!

Dear FYSA,

My agent told me that while I can expect some *publicity and marketing support from my publisher, I should plan to do a lot of the heavy lifting myself until my publicist is assigned. Uh … what does* that *mean?*

Yours,
Baffled in Brooklyn

Dear Baffled,

Well, it means exactly that: While a publishing house will provide a dedicated publicist for your book, they won't actually step onto the scene until three to six months before your book publishes. But there is much that can (and should) be done long before then. Here are some very basic steps to lay the groundwork in front of meeting your eventual publicity and marketing team:

1. **DOWNLOAD INSTAGRAM.** Use it to start looking for Bookstagrammers—folks who take stunning pics of books—who have hundreds of thousands of followers. Then make a list of the accounts you would like your publicist to target that fit the genre and aesthetic of your book.
2. **JOIN GOODREADS.** It's an influential community that your publisher can utilize in marketing. (Plus, it's really fun to explore.)
3. **NETWORK.** What people or organizations do you already have ties with that could potentially support your book upon publication? Reach out to alma mater newsletters, chat up your local bookstores, and attend local book festivals and conferences.
4. **IDENTIFY YOUR AUDIENCE.** Who will be reading your book? If you say, "All women between the ages of eighteen and ninety," then I'm going to go wait in the car, because we're done here. Really think about it, and then start making some assumptions. Are they men who also enjoy gardening? Are they women who are also into rock climbing? What shows would your reader watch? What online communities are they a part of? What podcasts do they listen to? When you can clearly identify your reader, you can discover where else in the world they are—and that is where you will find even more readers.

5. **KNOW HOW TO TALK ABOUT YOUR BOOK.** More than just the pitch and premise, understand how your novel fits into the current zeitgeist, whether it is a political intrigue or a generational novel about fly-fishing.

These simple steps can be done in your pajamas. (Well, maybe put on pants to go to the bookstore. But they can be, like, pajama jeans.) And by the time your publicist connects with you, you'll be fully prepared to participate in and facilitate certain avenues of pursuit for the team to create a foundation for a successful launch.

Dear FYSA,

If an editor wants me to transform my middle-grade novel into either a YA or adult novel because they think it will sell better—and even wants added content that goes against my personal beliefs—what should I do? If I refuse, is there a chance the editor would add those things in anyway, without me knowing?

Sincerely,
Paranoid in Paris

Dear Paranoid,

The good news is that at the point of sale, the intended audience for your novel will already have been established. While an agent—in a rare occasion—might submit to both middle-grade and YA editors if they feel both are applicable, by the time an offer from a publisher comes through you'll have a full understanding of where this book was intended to be placed, and can decide whether or not to move forward at that early moment. While occasionally an editor's enthusiasm for a novel can translate into heavy rounds of revisions, you'll receive drafts and proofs every step of the way prior to publication, so there's no real opportunity for your editor to squeak a major structural content shift past you.

But regarding content: Personal beliefs can be very … personal. And that's something I'm willing to respect and defend on behalf of my authors in these situations. One woman's *Lord of the Flies* is another woman's Judy Blume and all that. We all reserve the right to draw lines in the sand when it comes to our own work.

That said, these sorts of suggestions aren't made by your editor on a whim. What would typically happen here is the editor would call the *agent* and say, "Hey there, I love this manuscript, but because of (a) and (b) we're thinking it might be better suited for YA." These would be succinct and practical points. Then you and I discuss the category change and decide. You could say, "Nope!" and that's fine, but then we'd definitely want to explore the issues represented by (a) and (b) anyway, and see if there's a way to tweak the manuscript in order to ensure you aren't *missing* your intended middle-grade audience.

No one wants a manuscript to fall between shelves, but that shouldn't ever mean compromising your own integrity—and adding content that you feel goes against your intent, both personal and professional, is *not* the right solution. But neither is ignoring something in the manuscript that made your editor say, "Have you considered this?" So … consider.

Dear FYSA,

I'm having problems with my publisher and my agent always sides with them. All the time. And it got me thinking, does an agent have a better interest in keeping the publisher happy so that he can keep working with them with other projects? Is it foolish of me to think that my agent might choose them over me?

Sincerely,
Suspicions in Sunnyvale

Dear Suspicions,

First of all … is everything okay? Like, what is going on over there? Why are you having so many "problems" with your publishing team? Are they creative differences concerning revisions to your manuscript? Are they frustrations about turnaround times and delivery dates? Are they publicity and marketing issues? Or are they all traceable back to a single issue and these are just the after ripples? Also, I get a little cringey at the phrase "sides with" because we all have a common goal, we are all wearing the same jersey as we rush the field. Just because there are differences doesn't mean there are opposite sides. Your publisher is not your opponent; they are your partner.

And let's be clear, as an agent I am your advocate, but my job is not to get you everything you want. My job is to facilitate your career. And that sometimes includes pointing out when you are incorrect or misinformed in either a perception or a fact. That is not me taking a side, that is me continuing to keep you aware of the issues and their conclusions in order to make the smoothest and most successful publication path possible. My clients know I have a saying, "I am here to keep you happy and successful, but it won't always be in that order." Sometimes my clients need to hear me unpack for them that the hill they are trying to die to defend is nothing more than a pile of sand, and that is always a hard moment. Because they might feel like I am against them, but I am still and always *for* them. Yes, I have other books and careers rooted at that publishing house, and I would like to sell them more in the future, but being concerned about whether or not the publishers like me isn't even in my top ten.

But! These feelings you are having certainly are not occurring in a vacuum. I would recommend that you set up a time to have a call with your agent—*not* email, because tone can be misread in emails—and cite the recent occurrences where you felt your agent was keener on prioritizing the publisher over your concerns.

Dear FYSA,

I sold my first novel to a major house. That first novel did not sell well. My agent and I are about to offer my second book to the publisher, and I am really scared they will pass based on numbers, not content. Any words of wisdom?

Signed,
Second Shot

Dear Second Shot,

Preach, yo. This is something I am up against all the time. Not to clutch my cane and shake my fist, but back in my day I felt as if we had more than just the life of one book to build an author at a major house. (I also had to walk to work in the snow. Uphill. Both ways.) But these days it almost seems that we get one shot at the target, so we better blow it up. And when I say "we" I mean the publishing team as a whole.

The best thing to do—and prepare to grab your eyes if they actually roll right out of the sockets—is write a phenomenal second book. Like an *Empire Strikes Back* to your *Star Wars*. Here's a secret that is probably the reason there are so many forehead marks on my wall: If someone has the kind of follow-up book that gets them at "nerf herder" and keeps them until "I love you/I know," then we can steer into the idea of this being the breakout book.

Again, publishers will know the code-speak, because we have all been there, but there is hope for renewing a contract with a true breakout. Then we hit 'em with "I *am* your father."

The rest is all *yub nub, eee chop, yub nub.* (Yeah, I know the opening lyrics to the song "Ewok Celebration" at the end of *Return of the Jedi*. So what.)

Dear FYSA,

The planned publicity and marketing for my debut feels a little underwhelming. I would like to set up my own book tour. Is this a good idea?

Sincerely,
On the Road

Dear Roadie,

No matter what a publishing house secures an author for publicity and marketing, there is always more the author can be doing/building on to add to the campaign. That being said, sometimes the reasons a publisher decides against a certain avenue of pursuit in publicity or marketing is that they can't get the return of investment to make sense. And I would ask you to think this through on your own end before deciding a tour is a better investment than, say, purchased ads or a virtual or bookstagram tour.

As a debut, in the case of an actual city by city book tour, it is much harder to get folks to show up for an unknown, untested author—and compound that with a tour that takes place in tough weather climates, or during a holiday season, and you have a lot of dollars in flights and hotels, with not a lot of books being sold at the events.

However! If you already have a network of folks in a few cities where you *know* you can get thirty-five to fifty people on a Wednesday in Denver to come and buy a book, by all means! Set yourself up for a tour! First email your editor and publicist and let them know *why* you are confident you will get people to attend at each stop. Tell them about the cities you plan to tour, and what dates you will be in each city. Then ask your publicist to please reach out to bookstores to host each event, and ask them to tap into local media outreach. I would also suggest that you ask your editor if the imprint has other clients in the regions where you are touring. They can get a two-fer by having the two of you "in conversation" and you can also cross pollinate your audiences.

Dear FYSA,

What's the key to staying supportive of writer friends when they find more success than you do?

Signed,
PB & Jelly(ous)

Dear PB & J,

The publishing path is like a game of Plinko on *The Price Is Right*: You all have the same chip to drop in, but it won't take the same course to its destination. Try to find the confidence to assert that your boots are exactly where they need to be on *your* path. Know, too, that those chips can take a sudden wild hop—for better or for worse. One day you and your friend may have switched places, so it's wise to act the way you hope he might if and when that time comes.

You can't ever truly control a reflex of envy, but here are some hypothetical scenarios to keep you self-aware, outwardly projecting more of the PB (Positive Buddy) and less of the J.

Jelly: A friend emails to say the manuscript she sent out on Friday has an offer of representation. It's Monday.

PB: Burn a printed copy of that email over the kitchen sink while hissing, "*So glad I got that MFA.*" Then return to the computer and type, "Huge congrats! Let me know if you want to Skype with wine tonight so we can run through your list of questions to ask the agent." Bonus: It'll help you prep for your own eventual call, too.

Jelly: You've sold two books for $10,000 each. Your friend's debut just banked $250,000. Each. For a trilogy.

PB: Scream into a throw pillow until your spouse offers to take the kids out for dinner. When the house is quiet, call your friend and say, "My envy is as green as the Prada bag you will buy me for having helped you revise." She wants to buy you that bag, because without you, she never would have made the brother be the murderer. And what a *twist* that was.

Jelly: Your friend hit *The New York Times* list the week she debuted.

PB: Place your friend's book in the driveway and back over it. Then text her: "WOW! *So* happy for you! And for me, too, because now I know a bestseller who will blurb *my* book for my query letter to agents."

It's okay to acknowledge the green-eyed monster—just don't let him linger. Consider it fuel for the fire—then get back to focusing on your own Plinko chip.

Dear FYSA,

I'm having a really hard time writing my second book—how often do your clients ask for more time? And what is the average length they ask for?

Signed,
Deadline Dead End

Dear Deadline,

I hear ya—if only there were more hours in the day. So many flavored vodkas, so little time.

It *is* incredibly difficult to fit what is essentially an entire second career into an already busy life, especially when it is a career where creativity and inspiration have to strike—and those two don't keep banker's hours. The majority of authors faced with a blinking cursor on the empty first page of their second book feel exactly the way you do. I call it Sophomore Syndrome. (Just as pernicious as the Freshman Fifteen—and just as difficult to work off.)

There's a whole new set of rules for the second book, presuming it's the first you've written while already under contract: specific deadlines for delivery, perceived expectations from your agent and editor, and an invisible audience to recapture and expand with a fresh story. This is where discipline and dedication need to be your partners ... and where they can sometimes bolt for the door and leave you with the bill.

In part to open this question up to a broader audience, let's back up a second. There are several ways to get in front of this issue *before* you find yourself staring at your delivery date with only 30,000 words down and 60,000 to go. Let's address those first:

DIVIDE UP YOUR CALENDAR. When you have a contracted delivery date established, mark how far along your work-in-progress word count should be by the end of each month. (If the production schedule overlaps with that of your earlier book, ask your editor to share the book one schedule so that you can factor in times where you'll need to turn your attention back to that first project—to review copy edits and page proofs, do marketing pushes, etc.) If you start to sense you're falling behind in two consecutive months, this is the time to get more support from your personal life and borrow time to catch up. Book that babysitter, and trade a night at the big screen for a night at the computer screen. Ask a neighbor to double everything on her grocery list, throw some cash her way, and turn your shopping time into typing time.

(Bonus: Enjoy discovering what your neighbor buys at the grocery store. I mean, seriously … *herring*?) Wherever you can get support from partners and friends, start recruiting them to help you get that word count up and ahead.

CARRY A SMARTPHONE or even a good old pad of paper with you wherever you go. I promise you will find ten- and fifteen-minute increments throughout the day to jot down some words—and those add up. (My client *New York Times* bestseller Michelle Gable wrote most of her second book, *I'll See You in Paris*, longhand on legal pads while waiting for her daughters' at-bats during softball tournaments!)

HOLD YOURSELF ACCOUNTABLE to family and friends when opportunities arise. Get a cheering section, not a jeering section, when you have to show up late. "I would love to meet you tonight at Sharky's Chum & Ale House, so as soon as I get my two thousand words down I'll be there!" Incentivize yourself to get it done without missing out on *all* of the fun.

ASK YOUR LIFE PARTNER TO RUN THE SHOW with the kids one night a week—without risking a call to 1-800-DIVORCE—and seek out someplace quiet where you can plug in and type without distraction.

Which, all told, brings us to this fact: Life happens. Especially when you have day jobs and family and chaos. So if you are doing all of these things and still need an extension, the time to discuss this with your agent is four to five weeks before your deadline, *not* a day before.

My clients rarely ask for more time—mainly because they are total beasts. I love them. Ultimately, they've all been very lucky with their health and safety, and the health and safety of those they love, holding steady during pinch delivery times. But it's also rare for them to have to *ask* for an extension because we are in such constant contact. In casual conversation I'll do my best to say things like, "You okay with that June delivery still?" or, "Remember, this deadline falls right after the holidays." Be honest with your agent and let her get in front of the problem before it *becomes* a problem; that is the next line of defense to protect your delivery.

When I do get my folks more time, it's usually three weeks or fewer. Sometimes just the knowledge that they *have* more time ends up allowing an author to meet the original deadline after all. There are also occasions in which I know that certain authors are inclined to use those additional weeks to obsess over every page—which isn't healthy—so I'll actually deny their request. There's always something else to revise, and if that means I have to get out the wooden broomstick and knock them off the electrical current of their book I'll do it.

The big takeaway here is that we are all busy, we are all easily distracted. There are so very many opportunities to *not* write that next book, but taking the steps to buckle down before it becomes a delivery issue is your greatest offense.

That being said, get back to work. I'll see you at Sharky's—*after* you get your words done. Chum's on me.

Dear FYSA,

What advice would you give to a client who has finished and delivered their first novel to their publisher but is stumped about what to write next?

Signed,
The Well Is Dry

Dear Well Is Dry,

When my clients are short on ideas for what to write next, what I like to do is point at my shoes and scream, "What, you think these Prada wedges just *happen*?" And then I find a processed-meat product and throw it through a plate-glass window to punctuate the outburst. Over a dozen years in the biz and that strategy hasn't failed me yet!

But what's *also* helpful is to remember that stories don't just happen in a book vacuum, but are taking shape in all forms of media and out in that ol' third dimension of real life as well. There's a whole world to be mined for character and conflict. Even a leisurely walk in the city, tuning in to bits of conversation, can be a catalyst. The key here is to release the pressure of opening a blank document, staring at the blinking cursor and thinking, *I have to write a book*. Here are some of my favorite prompts to get clients' think-stews all bubbly:

- Dig a box of photos out of storage, or pull out an old album. Find a picture that has an object in it and make that a charged object in a short story.
- Take your favorite antagonist in any film or novel and write a scene where they are the hero.
- Learn to meditate. (Hey, don't knock it till you *om* it.)
- Get co-workers/family members/friends to share their most embarrassing moments (be ready to reciprocate!), and write a short story based on one from the POV of your choice.
- Binge-watch The History Channel. (*Dateline* works too!)
- Flip to page 108 of any novel, take the first full sentence and use it as the opening line of your own short story.

These are creative exercises I've used in writing classes, as well as with my clients. As in any exercise, the idea is to stimulate movement in the mind and just get words on the page. That blank document doesn't have to be your next opus—it just has to keep the current flowing until you find that one piece of driftwood and hang on for the ride.

Dear FYSA,

I always hear about how valuable writers' conferences can be, and how being on panels can help sales of my books, but the idea of showing up by myself to a four-day conference is greatly intimidating. How can I overcome this?

Best,
Timid in Tampa

Dear Timid,

You *know* I just want to say, "vodka," and mic drop . . . but this is a family show.

Instead, I want to acknowledge that you feel intimidated and uncomfortable. Conferences aren't for everyone, and I'm all for you finding a realm of similar value that doesn't require you stay in a hotel with strangers, load your pockets with Xanax and white-knuckle through small talk. There are some *fabulous* online forums out there that provide fertile soil for planting seeds of education and camaraderie that mimic the experience of attending an in-person event.

For example, I'm a fan of the online classes taught through The Loft Literary Center in Minneapolis. In fact, I once taught an online course there (and through said course, signed and sold Kaethe Schwehn's *The Rending and the Nest* to Bloomsbury—which goes to show, web-based courses can reap professional rewards, too). That class environment was so supportive that many of those students still keep in touch and meet up when they can. And they definitely buy each other's books.

That being said, there is an insensitive, shouty version of me that wants to yell at you to put aside the insecurity and *just do it!* Of course, *my* threshold for timid is only slightly below inebriated St. Bernard, so what if we split the difference and focus on finding you a local conference? One that's craft-centered, with multiple daily opportunities to teach and speak, but also to enhance and expand not only your writing, but your writing *circle* by surrounding you with folks from your region who share the same goals. To name a few, Mystery Writers of America, Sisters in Crime, and Romance Writers of America are all organizations that have local chapters. Do some Googling.

But if you do change your mind and want to cannonball in, a couple of my favorite national events are ThrillerFest and the Writer's Digest Annual Conference [*Editor's Note: We didn't tell her to say this, we swear!*]. I've found the attendees and support staff to be knowledgeable, inclusive, and very user-friendly. Added bonus: I'm usually lurking around those two conferences as well, so if you see me you can shout "Hashtag Cannonball!" and we can high-five. I'm told high-fives are key to overcoming intimidation.

Dear FYSA,

I'm a debut author under contract, and while I'm thrilled for my book to publish in a year, I'm concerned about how many books like mine are popping up in the meantime. Will the publisher cancel my book if there are too many others like it?

Sincerely,
Category Claustrophobia

Dear Claustrophobia,

I can totally understand your trepidation. If you were a client at my agency (and I believe this holds true for most agencies), I'd tell you that we negotiated a clause in your publishing contract that prevents this particular situation from being cause to cancel. The publishing calendar is a crystal ball of sorts: The things that I'm selling today won't see shelf space until eighteen to twenty-four months from now. We thus have to take current trends into consideration, but the caveat is that no one really knows how long a trend or subgenre will dominate, because we are selling this year when, say, YA fantasy is at a peak, but the tide may start to wane. The good news is that publishers know this, and a savvy agent also knows the right language to include in a contract to avoid an outright cancellation.

Dear FYSA,

What are your favorite productivity hacks from high-volume clients?

Sincerely,
Seeking Shortcuts

Dear Shorty,

Ah yes, the age-old question: How do I get the most by doing the verrrrry least? It's basically my Zen kōan.

Oh, how I wish I could say, "Well, since you asked, there is this secret code you can enter into any Word document that writes your novel for you while you binge-watch Netflix and eat pastries." Alas, lift your sticky fingers from the keys—no such code exists. A writer writes. That's how the words happen. Ain't no hacking there except away at the pages. And that, my friend, is how high-volume authors produce all those books at such a ferocious clip.

However! Being a writer is one thing; being a *published author* is another. There are a few *author* hacks that I've found valuable to clients, but they usually come in the form of support staff. You might have taken four years or more to write the novel that finally got you a book deal, but once you enter into the publishing machine, you're going to need to churn out those fancy-worded, highfalutin tomes on the regular every twelve to eighteen months—all the while doing the editing, publicity, and the support for the book that preceded it. That is where publicists can be a fabulous WWE (Writers With Exhaustion) partners—tag 'em in!

Bringing in an outside publicist—like Dana Kaye of Kaye Publicity, someone I see on my clients' payroll all the time—who can create a plan for you to follow which details the best way to allot your time and focus will return *so much* sand to your hourglass. That way, while your publicist is funneling your attention toward your largest ROIs, you're able to turn back and continue your flop-sweat panic about how stalled out you are on book four … until you decide to tap in a Plot Doc!

A "plot doctor" (also called a developmental editor) is someone you can hire to help define what your book is about and identify ways to move it forward. Lemme say, I have seen some truly *amazing* results with folks like Adrienne Bell and her Plot MD services, which usually require the author to fill out a series of questionnaires about their work and then hop on the phone for a consultation call. This can save days of staring—slack jawed and terrified—at that fickle mistress of a cursor that's winking seductively at you from the empty page.

And the final hack? An assistant. Despite your preconceived notions, you don't have to be Fancy Pants McGillicuddy to have an assistant. (Though McGillicuddy's assistants all have their *own* assistants who do wear actual fancy pants, or so I've heard.) The application of assistants can range from four hours a week for email and social media management to twenty hours a week for research and calendar/tour management and beyond. I suggest reaching out and placing ads on job boards where local college students will see them—those folks will be pleased to get the experience, and *you* will be pleased to have someone to wipe all the pastry flakes off your desk.

Dear FYSA,

Someone in my writers' group is at the same publisher as I am. We write in similar genres, we are about to have our third books published. Lately she is passive aggressively making comparisons about our careers, her advance, what the publisher is doing for me versus what they are doing for her, and it is causing tension in the group. And also, secretly, why I am writing to you? It is working. I am starting to feel like she is getting the best of everything. What do I do?

Sincerely,
She's Under My Skin

Dear Skinny,

[Opens bottom desk drawer.] [Bends down out of sight.] [Straightens up.] [Expressionless, presses air horn in an ear shattering bray.] [Bends down.] [Straightens up.] [Places megaphone in front of mouth.] [Slight feedback.]

"KEEP. YOUR. EYES. ON. YOUR. OWN. PAPER."

Every story is different, right? And careers themselves are stories. So why would any career be the same? Every single one of my authors has these days. Every. Single. One. Where someone is getting more of something, whether it is an advance or a marketing placement or publicity angle. Sometimes I get angry emails. Sometimes I get weepy phone calls. Sometimes both.

The world teaches us at a young age that there is only one first place in whatever we are competing in. However, that is just not the case in publishing. Someone can get an advance of $40K, earn it out in the first six months, and get five figure royalty checks for the next four years, while someone else got a six figure advance and then … that was it.

Who is first place there?

Someone could hit the *Times* list first week of publication with twenty-three hundred copies sold and then drop off to 250 a week for a few months and then seventy-five copies a week the rest of the year, then vanish, while someone else could *never* hit the list, but sell fifty-two thousand copies in their first year.

Who is first place there?

Someone could get on the *Today* show and sell fifteen hundred books that day, someone else could speak at their sorority alumni event, sell four hundred copies, and then get asked to tour college campuses and speak at their house events and sell 250 copies per visit over fifteen visits.

Who is first place there?

Someone could have Barnes and Noble request four thousand copies of a special signed edition of the their novel, and the publisher ends up shipping ten thousand total to all vendors, while someone else gets an initial order of two thousand copies from B&N, two book clubs of fourteen hundred each, three subscription boxes of 900 each, and an indie order of six thousand.

Who is first place there?

You are not going to get everything you want, not in life and certainly not in publishing. And I can 100 percent guarantee you she isn't either. And—color yourself shocked—she might be exaggerating what she *is* getting. But even if she isn't—you keep your eyes on your own paper. Tell your agent you feel needy and scared. Ask specific questions about things you'd like to see/have. Be prepared to hear, "You're not there yet." Or "The Publisher didn't budget for that." But at least you'll get them out there.

And let's be honest, anyone who is pass-agging at you is *terrified* of you for some reason. Next time she says something, what if you went totally bananas on her and just told your truth? "Gosh, it sounds like you are crushing it. It's fun to have you ahead of the rest of us to pave the way. I still feel nervous sometimes. Can I ask you a few questions? Like, what is the one thing you still wish our publisher was doing for you? What is your one dream 'get'?" Turn the conversation away from what she has and into a learning experience of what is still out there to get. That way you all can all scribble madly on your papers, too excited about what's still out there to peep at anyone else's.

Dear FYSA,

Recently I was at a coffee shop and noticed almost every individual there was glued to their handheld device. At a time when people don't seem to want to read anything longer than a text message, what hope does the future hold for good old-fashioned books? What is even the point anymore?

Yours,
Digitally Depressed

Dear Depressed,

What was that? I was busy watching this hilarious YouTube video of a monkey washing a cat. Let me just say ... *Whoops!* Sorry about that—had to check my MovUrBootz app which is telling me I need to take forty-seven more steps in the next three minutes to earn a golden cherry. (After three golden cherries I can do one less flight of stairs a day and *that* means ...)

Ack! Husband just texted me: "Do we have any mustard?" I know he's standing in front of the fridge, but let me just use my FridgeFriend app and text my refrigerator. Okay, bear with me real quick as I text him back, "Hey Siri, text Husband 'Yes—we have mustard.'" What? No, I didn't say, "Text Husband he's a turd." Back to it ... *Oh!* Calendar alert—tonight I'm going to FaceTime my bestie in Los Angeles for a wine date and I have to pick up some white Bordeaux. Anywhooziers, what the heck were you saying?

Totally relatable, right? Maybe you laughed, felt sheepish, recognized yourself, reflected on society. A little satire, a little comedy, a little character, a little thought. Now imagine that—but longer—with more laughs, more recognition, more reflection. That's a story. That's a book. And that's the point.

Conclusion

Well, there you have it. We've had a few laughs, maybe a few screams into a pillow, maybe a cocktail or eleven, but I hope we've done some learning. And I hope it is clear to you that I love my job. I love every part of it. And whooo boy I hope it is also clear that I am not perfect at it. And that some of my days are *just* as hard as yours, if not harder. Sometimes I am flying above the turbulence with a drink in my hand and a song in my heart and sometimes I am a clown falling down a spiral staircase, just beeps and honks and bleeding. But I am so lucky and so honored to have this career. The facilitation of art. The discovery of new talent, the dealing, the schmoozing, the lunches, dinners, cocktails. The knowing that every book I broker will change lives—not just the readers' but the authors' as well. And oh, how I love the calls—calls about covers and reviews. Calls about list placement or list absence. Calls where I pitch. Calls filled with dollars. Calls filled with laughter, big fat throw-back-your-head-and-cackle laughter. Calls filled with tears. Calls where I murmur, calls where I bray, calls where I soothe, and calls where I fire up.

But as a literary agent, my two most very favorite calls to make are the call to sign the author and the call to tell the author we have an offer on their work. And these calls can sometimes be days apart … or years apart. The offer can be on the manuscript with which I signed them, or it can be on the third or fourth manuscript I shopped. There has to be that electric spark of right time/right book that creates that conduit, but above all else right *talent*.

The writing has to be phenomenal in craft, technique, and narrative voice. And that has to start from page one.

Actually, paragraph one. Actually *line* one.

I am now going to tell you what you've been waiting for this entire book: The secret formula that will ensure you not only sign an agent, but have that six-figure book deal in hand by your next birthday …

And if you believe that? I have some *stunning* swampland down in Florida I'd like to sell you as well.

Because, sadly, there isn't a formula. If there were, I would be dictating this book to my butler as he unwraps each of my Bit-O-Honey candies poolside in Turks and Caicos. The only ingredient I can tell you that exists in *every* author stew? They didn't give up. They just didn't. So why would you?

Now go forth into the breach my friend and write! Write like the wind!

Because now? Now the real work begins.

Agent Worksheet

Download this as a printable worksheet at www.writersdigest.com/funny-you-should-ask-book.

1. Make a spreadsheet of thirty agents you will query, including their specific requirements for query submission. (i.e. this agent wants just a query, this agent want a query and the first ten pages all in the body of the email, etc.). You can find these agents using internet sites like Query Shark (queryshark.blogspot.com), or you can get something like *Guide to Literary Agents*, or you can head to your library or bookstore and hang out in your genre and pluck titles off of the shelf and flip to the acknowledgments and see who the author thanked. That's a good indication that the agent is acquiring this type of material.
2. *Have a complete and ready-to-rock manuscript before you begin to query.* There is nothing more frustrating for an agent to request a manuscript and hear, "I should be finished with my initial draft in September, will send it along!" I don't want a draft of anything. And I probably will have already filled my list with new clients that *were* prepared.
3. Get your query letter in order—remember this is your book's job interview. You want it to be professional and well appointed, make it smooth and easy to say "yes" to seeing the pages.

   REMEMBER MY SECRET RECEIPE: the hook, the book, the cook. The hook is the opening log line of your book along with word count, genre, and any comp titles. The book is four to five lines of premise—*not plot!*—and then the cook is ... you! Three or four lines about why this book, why you, why now. Even if you wrote this novel out longhand first between your kids' softball games, it isn't going to hurt you; you just need to give an idea of your background.

4. Make sure you are querying both fresh, new agents and old standbys. Lots of ways to skin a stegosaurus, and remember, even yours truly was once a baby agent in knock off Keds offering on a client for the first time. And now I am running around in fabulous shoes skinning stegosauruses.

QUESTIONS TO ASK AN AGENT OFFERING REPRESENTATION

- How much editorial work do you foresee before this is ready to be shopped? Can you tell me specifics on what you will be asking to revise?
- How do you shop rights like foreign and film? Do you use sub agents?
- What is the agency culture like in your offices? Are your clients connecting with, supporting, and helping promote each other and/or clients of other agents in your agency? Can you give me any examples?
- How long have you been with the agency and what steps would need to be taken if you left the agency to continue our contract?
- How do you prefer to communicate? Will I always be communicating with you or does an assistant handle day to day questions?

- What is your average response time on email?
- May I please speak with two of your clients?

WHEN YOU CONNECT WITH THE CLIENTS, ASK

- What is one thing you think the agent does very well?
- What is one thing you think she could improve upon?
- What was your biggest surprise on your path to getting published?

Poelle Publishing Bingo!

Please choose one of seven cards to hang up in your writing space. (Feel free to give the others to CPs!) As you plunge ahead on you publishing path, machete swinging, pith helmet at a rakish angle, take the time to mark off the milestones. When you achieve a Bingo, do something nice for yourself: go hit a bucket of balls, get a manicure, buy that autographed picture of Yasmine Bleeth you've been eyeing on eBay. When you have a blackout Bingo card, take the time to live in that moment, and then find someone at the beginning and offer them your ear, your advice, and your pith helmet.

Download this as a printable worksheet at www.writersdigest.com/funny-you-should-ask-book.

The book is awful, I am a failure	On submission to editors!	2,000 words today!	First revisions returned to editor	PUB DAY!
Book going to auction	Completed full draft of manuscript	First author panel at conference	Finished final draft	Book didn't sell to publishers
15 Rejections	On submission to agents!	Free!	Was assigned a pub date	Multiple agent offers
Three chapters in on next book	Signed my first copy for reader	Someone asks why I don't self pub	First blurb in	Lame book dominates NYT list
I think I might actually be good at this	Full manuscript request!	Got 5K followers on social platform	Signed with an agent!	CP gets book deal

Signed my first copy for reader	Three chapters in on next book	PUB DAY!	Book didn't sell to publishers	Book going to auction
On submission to editors!	2,000 words today!	Multiple agent offers	Lame book dominates NYT list	Signed with an agent!
First author panel at conference	First revisions returned to editor	Free!	First blurb in	On submission to agents!
Was assigned a pub date	Completed full draft of manuscript	CP gets book deal	I think I might actually be good at this	Someone asks why I don't self pub
Full manuscript request!	Got 5K followers on social platform	The book is awful, I am a failure	15 rejections	Finished final draft

Someone asks why I don't self pub	On submission to Agents!	PUB DAY!	Three chapters in on next book	First revisions returned to editor
Signed my first copy for reader	I think I might actually be good at this	2,000 words today!	Multiple agent offers	Finished final draft
Book going to auction	The book is awful, I am a failure	Free!	Was assigned a pub date	Lame book dominates NYT list
15 rejections	First author panel at conference	Got 5K followers on social platform	Signed with an agent!	On submission to editors !
Book didn't sell to publishers	Full manuscript request!	CP gets book deal	First blurb in	Completed full draft of manuscript

On submission to agents!	Signed with an agent!	Book going to auction	15 rejections	First revisions returned to editor
First blurb in	First author panel at conference	Finished final draft	Someone asks why I don't self pub	2,000 words today!
CP gets book deal	I think I might actually be good at this	Free!	On submission to editors!	Completed full draft of manuscript
Three chapters in on next book	Lame book dominates NYT list	PUB DAY!	Book didn't sell to publishers	Got 5K followers on social platform
The book is awful, I am a failure	Signed my first copy for reader	Full manuscript request!	Was assigned a pub date	Multiple agent offers

Got 5K followers on social platform	CP gets book deal	Book going to auction	Signed with an agent!	Three chapters in on next book
I think I might actually be good at this	15 rejections	The book is awful, I am a failure	Completed full draft of manuscript	First revisions returned to editor
Full manuscript request!	On submission to editors!	Free!	Was assigned a pub date	Someone asks why I don't self pub
Multiple agent offers	Signed my first copy for reader	Book didn't sell to publishers	PUB DAY!	First author panel at conference
On submission to agents!	Finished final draft	Lame book dominates NYT list	First blurb in	2,000 words today!

On submission to Agents!	Someone asks why I don't self pub	Book going to auction	Lame book dominates NYT list	First revisions returned to editor
Three chapters in on next book	Signed with an agent!	Full manuscript request!	Completed full draft of manuscript	Got 5K followers on social platform
2,000 words today!	First author panel at conference	Free!	Finished final draft	The book is awful, I am a failure
First blurb in	Signed my first copy for reader	15 rejections	Book didn't sell to publishers	PUB DAY!
On submission to editors!	Multiple agent offers	CP gets book deal	Was assigned a pub date	I think I might actually be good at this

Got 5K followers on social platform	First author panel at conference	Multiple agent offers	First blurb in	I think I might actually be good at this
CP gets book deal	Signed with an agent!	PUB DAY!	2000 words today!	Lame book dominates NYT list
First revisions returned to editor	The book is awful, I am a failure	Free!	On submission to agents!	Finished final draft
Signed my first copy for reader	On submission to editors!	Someone asks why I don't self pub	Completed full draft of manuscript	Was assigned a pub date
Book going to auction	Three chapters in on next book	Book didn't sell to publishers	15 rejections	FULL manuscript request!

Reader, Writer, Consumer Worksheet

Do not read this worksheet until you read a new book—and make it one that you have been meaning to read. Once you turn the final page, you may begin. Find a place to sit and either with pen and paper or on a screen, take the time to consider and respond to each question. Each section should take less than fifteen minutes—this isn't the SATs. We are training your brain to read books in ways that help you define what works and what doesn't and *why* you feel this way.

Download this as a printable worksheet at www.writersdigest.com/funny-you-should-ask-book.

READING LIKE A READER

1. What "hooked" me about this book? Why did I want to keep reading? Or why didn't I?
2. How well did I relate to the characters and their motivations? Did the book feel well suited to my expectations?
3. Would I read another book by this author? Why?

READING LIKE A WRITER

1. How much work did the first sentence do to accomplish what it needed to in order to hook the reader? The first chapter?

2. What did I learn about the protagonists in the first ten pages, and how was the information conveyed? Was there any aspect of the protagonist that I didn't expect to relate to but did? Why? How was the antagonist identified as such?
3. How quickly were the "beats" coming in each scene? What one word would I use to describe the pacing? What's one take-away from the arc and escalation of the individual scenes that I can use in my own writing? Was there any part of the book that made me exhale and murmur, "How did she *do* that?" Why?

READING LIKE A CONSUMER

1. What was the mitigating factor in my choice of book?
2. What about the packaging was appealing? What wasn't?
3. How would I compare the packaging to others in the genre? Would I be more likely to remember the author's name or the title?

Getting Started 24 in 24

GOAL: By the end of this exercise you will have twenty-four story premises.

DIRECTIONS: Come up with twenty-four titles for possible novels and then develop a four to five line premise supporting the title. You should complete this exercise in no more than twenty-four hours. *Do not overthink it.* But know, that the moment you write the first idea, the clock starts and you have twenty-four hours to write the last.

Download this as a printable worksheet at www.writersdigest.com/funny-you-should-ask-book.

TITLE	FOUR TO FIVE SENTENCE PREMISE

TITLE	FOUR TO FIVE SENTENCE PREMISE

TITLE	FOUR TO FIVE SENTENCE PREMISE

WRITING EXERCISE 2

Finding the Pivot Using Character Construction

Remember, people want to read characters' choices leading to action. Not action informing characters' choices. Finding nuances and layers to your characters can help bolster scenes that may otherwise be reading flat.

Download this as a printable worksheet at www.writersdigest.com/funny-you-should-ask-book.

List ten traits about your protagonist that won't ever be in the book. For example, my protagonist only wears black underwear, won't eat at restaurants with four or more negative reviews on Yelp, once saw a ghost, etc. ...

1.
2.
3.
4.
5.
6.
7.
8.
9.
10.

Write a scene in which your protagonist does each of these things (separate scenes or all at once, your choice):

1. Fires a gun.
2. Answers a door.
3. Lies.

Write a scene where a charged object appears. How does the object help to reveal the protagonist's character? What else seems important about this object as a story device?

Setting as a mirror: Write a scene where the protagonist is entering a location that reflects their mental state—the room as a metaphor.

Take a pivotal scene and, in your mind's eye, look around and see someone unnamed in the setting: maybe a bar patron, a bus rider, a woman in a park, and write an inner monologue from their POV about what is happening in the scene.

WRITING EXERCISE 3

Loosening the Sticking Place

Download this as a printable worksheet at www.writersdigest.com/funny-you-should-ask-book.

1. Rewrite the final conflict scene between the protagonist and antagonist from the antagonist's POV where *they* are the hero/protagonist.
2. Take a famous scene from a classic or bestselling novel and write your protagonist into the chapter, keeping them grounded in their construct.
3. Take the scene with the catalyst before the catharsis in your novel and *change a key decision* that your protagonist makes.

INDEX